THE WRITING PROJECT

The Writing Project

RECOVERING THE WRITING SELF AND REGAINING AGENCY THROUGH WRITING ABOUT DOMESTIC ABUSE

STACEY ANWIN

Vivre Books

© Stacey Anwin 2024

The right of Stacey Anwin to be identified as author of this work has been asserted in accordance with sections 77 and 78 of the Copyright, Designs and Patents Act 1988.

All rights reserved. No part of this book may be reprinted or reproduced or utilised in any form or by any electronic, mechanical, or other means, now known or hereafter invented, including photocopying and recording, or in any information storage or retrieval system, without permission in writing from the author.

Epigraph on p.v © Ana Åberg 2022, used with permission.

A Cataloguing-in-Publication entry for this work is available from the National Library of Australia

ISBN 978-1-7635359-0-9 (paperback)
ISBN 978-1-7635359-1-6 (ebook)

Design and typography copyright © Stacey Anwin 2024
Cover image of colourful bird in flight © Conrad Roset, used with permission.

Vivre Books

She values, above all else, freedom. Though she lives in a cage, she sings with the almightiest of voices, the sound carrying on the wind into the fields, across the river to the forest beyond.

Excerpt from 'her voice, her freedom', Ana Åberg

Contents

A NOTE TO YOU, MY READER

Introduction	1
Chapter 1 Creative Nonfiction	8
Chapter 2 Dramatic Monologue	32
Chapter 3 Young Adult Fiction	45
Chapter 4 Poetry	75
Chapter 5 Fairy Tale	90
Chapter 6 Essential Pause	107
Chapter 7 Trauma Writing	116
Chapter 8 Horror	123
Chapter 9 Whispers	140
Chapter 10 Diary Entries	152
Chapter 11 L'écriture Féminine	170
Chapter 12 Writing As Strategy	183
Conclusion	211
Notes	217

A NOTE TO YOU, MY READER

Dear Reader,

This book discusses domestic abuse. You may find some of this to be confronting, disturbing or upsetting. As the reader, you are entirely in control of how much you read, when, and how. When I read memoirs that speak of violence and abuse, I may skip over pages, leaving them unread. This is my means of persisting with a story while protecting myself. I do not deny the author's story in doing so; I simply understand my capacity and limits. I ask you to consider also setting boundaries when reading memoirs that discuss trauma. In doing so, you enact the power that is yours as reader.

Yours sincerely,

Stacey

Dear Reader,

Introduction

Key Concepts

I have always believed in the power of the written word. From an early age, I read and took notes, eager to learn. I dreamt of going to university to read more, to learn more, to become one of those who also put pen to paper, who used their education to elicit positive social change. For me, to write was to be empowered. While I enjoyed writing to fulfill certain tasks, closer to my heart was my personal creative writing practice, my *writing for the self*. This writing was integral to my self-identity.

The Writing Project is an account of my journey from a place of loss to a place of hope. When I began, I had trauma induced writing block. That is, I had lost my ability to write for myself and of the self. I call this complete creative writing block.

By 'creative', I mean only my creative written expression was affected; I continued to write otherwise, for academic, legal or transactional purposes. By 'complete', I mean I lost not only my ability to think or write creatively, but also my drive to create. It was as if a synapse had been severed.

The influences in our developmental years contribute to the formation of our personalities, aspirations, values and behaviours.

Some of these are easily identifiable. In my case, the ability to read and write (with access to books and writing tools), was one such influence. Some influences are less clearly identifiable, such as those embedded in the broader culture in which we live, and in the micro-culture of our families. One such influence for me, the one that contributed greatly to my personality and behaviours, was domestic abuse. Domestic abuse can be physical, sexual, emotional, psychological, financial, spiritual or social.[1] I use the term domestic abuse, and not domestic violence, in line with the United Nations. As Yasmin Kahn, scholar and advocate states, 'words matter'.[2] Using the term domestic abuse makes it clear that physical violence is not the only form of abuse in the home and intimate relationships.

My writing for the self had been a life-long companion. A source of solace, it was my most reliable, accessible means of grappling with life's difficulties. It was a safe space for expressing emotions and playfulness when my outer life restricted these. It was a venue for righting wrongs; a means of enabling voice. During my years of complete creative writing block, my thoughts, feelings and responses had no outlet. Instead of moving onto a page, allowing processing, they putrefied within me.

My plan for overcoming this debilitating condition, complete creative writing block, was this: to write my way back into writing.

Regaining my personal writing practice meant relearning how to engage with the creative writing process in its most basic form. This involved firstly harnessing a desire to write, then imagining and compiling ideas. I could not progress into the actual writing stage of the process without these fundamental elements.

My approach was to conduct scaffolded writing experiments, exploring a selected genre and/or form in an attempt to enter the

INTRODUCTION

creative writing process. My hope was that, through trying out and trying on different genres and forms, I would reconnect with my creative writing self: to once again, write for myself in my everyday life. And this did occur. As I reconnected with my creativity, my reliance on the scaffolding diminished. Eventually, instead of relying on the support of a guiding structure, I began to write freely. From there, the experiments drew naturally to a conclusion.

Integral to the success of this project was my choice of writing topic: domestic abuse. It was the topic I most needed to write about but could not. Domestic abuse is not aberrant behaviour that occurs 'elsewhere', nor is it uncommon: in Australia, over a million women are directly affected.[3] How can we ignore the murders of women, between 40 and 52 a year, by men who were, or had been, their partners?[4] If I could not write about this topic to help myself, perhaps I could do so with the goal of offering stories for others to connect with. This goal acted as compelling motivation to participate in the writing experiments.

My journey from complete creative writing block to *at-will* written expression, was slow. I drew on many strategies and resources to help me, including enrolling in a research degree to create accountability. Being able to write about, and write my way through, some of my experiences of domestic abuse has made it possible to gain new perspectives on my life, thus developing understanding, wisdom and the opportunity to heal. I end my journey having returned from the land of the dead with the lost treasure: my ability to draw on my writing when I want, where I want, how I want. My writing, this intensely satisfying creative outlet for all that I feel, for all that I dream, allows me to respond to life again with power, with agency.

THE WRITING PROJECT

The following account of my journey was written contemporaneously with each writing experiment. The early chapters are therefore written from the perspective of the old me, the formerly blocked me, the person who did not know if she would recover her ability to write creatively at-will. I have maintained the integrity of that experience by keeping the tenses true to the story, my story, as it took place. I invite you, dear reader, to share this journey with me.

I have included samples of the extemporaneous writing that sprung from the experiments. Like the mending of broken bones signals physical healing, these extracurricular writing attempts signal the renewing of my creative self.

Finally, the Reflections sections were written well after the completion of the experiments. They represent my current perspective as the writer/researcher with a personal writing practice who exists because of this writing project. In these, I highlight and expand on insights gained through the writing experiments, particularly as regards agency and domestic abuse.

INTRODUCTION

Key concepts

Writer for the self

A person who writes only for herself. This personal writing includes any and all forms/genres/styles of writing. It is not limited to diary writing or journal keeping.

Writing block

'Writing block', or 'writer's block', is when a person who has the ability to write is unable to do so. Writing block is often incorrectly used to describe any impediment to writing, such as inadequate understanding of the appropriate writing conventions, or a lack of content knowledge. The writing block I discuss in this book, in contrast, is related to the impact of trauma on self-expression and voice.

A person may experience block in one style of writing, such as creative writing, but continue to write in other ways, such as business writing.

The creative writing process

Typically, this is shown to have three key stages:
- pre-writing (idea generation, planning)
- writing (drafting, redrafting) and
- post-writing (revising, editing, proofing).

The elements of these stages are not fixed in order: a writer may revise as they write; idea generation can occur while drafting. The writing process, however, is inaccessible to the person with complete creative writing block.

A fundamental step needs to be added for the writer for the self who is completely blocked: **desire** (impetus, motivation). Without this step, there can be no engagement in the writing process.

Writing experiments

These experiments, recorded in each chapter, follow the structure of exploring a genre and form. This structure guides attempts at engaging in the creative writing process.

Extemporaneous writing

Creative writing that occurs external to the defined writing experiments. The extemporaneous writing is evidence of at-will writing, that is, writing resulting from inner drive.

INTRODUCTION

Complete creative writing block

Chapter 1 Creative Nonfiction

Experiment 1 (June-November 2015)
Extemporaneous writing
Reflections

Writing for the self is a powerful writing practice. It is welcoming, encouraging, and offers endless possibilities. Writing for the self is free from judgment and restrictions. Through writing, we create a place to be more; to say, feel and live more.

In the past, I confidently wrote however and whatever I wanted. I wrote how the mood took me according to context, desire, or need. The freedom to write in and through a variety of genres and forms, voices and styles, was akin to having access to a private wellness spring, armoury, laboratory and artist's palette. My writing tools were sometimes healing potions and poultices. Sometimes, they were weapons and shields. Sometimes, they were instruments of navigation and discovery. And always, they were the means of creative expression. To write was to refresh and renew, to heal and to grow. To transform. It therefore seems natural to draw on a range of forms and genres, both fiction and nonfiction, for my experiments.

I begin my experiments with nonfiction, setting the task of writing a short feature story on domestic abuse. I think of such a piece as being brief enough to read while waiting for an appointment. Attempting a short, fact-driven piece sounds possible. And yet, where I am starting from is an empty space, devoid of the urge to write. As I cast about for ideas, they vanish at my touch. As I consider the task, it falls flat from lack of impetus.

To ease myself into the task, I examine how to write a feature story incorporating personal experience. However, as with many tasks, the preparation becomes a source of distraction. I feed the excuse of believing I need to read, read, read. To find suitable samples of where writers use their own experiences to create discussion of a larger issue and analyse style, technique, outcomes. After all, this is the approach taken to the teaching of writing, one that I also taught to my students. Find good examples of the genre, identify what makes them so, and emulate.

······

Months later, I have read many feature stories, analysed and taken notes. Still, I am unable to implement what I have learned. This is the emptiness of complete creative writing block. What I need to do, more than anything else, is write.

I decide to do a warmup exercise. Something to get my pencil moving across the page. An activity to stimulate, or perhaps, simulate, writing. I will write in the style of a tabloid news story. Short, direct. While this cannot be classified as expressive writing, it does involve writing from my personal experience. Here is the result:

A 38-year-old Brisbane woman has been attacked and sexually assaulted in her own home.

At around 8:30 last night, a woman called 000 to report the attack.

By the time police and police dogs arrived at the scene, the attacker had fled.

The woman claims her head had been bashed repeatedly against the tiles of her bathroom floor before being forced into the bathtub where she was sexually assaulted. Police state the woman identified the man, but they were not pursuing charges.

'The victim's facial injuries are not significantly evident to convince a jury there was an assault,' the Senior Detective said.

Ambulance officers attending the woman at the scene said she was dazed and confused, complaining of severe pain at the back of her head.

The woman claims she had been about to take a shower when the power was cut. She said her attacker was waiting outside the bathroom door in the dark.

Police have dismissed the matter as a domestic issue.

'He says, she says,' stated the Detective called to the scene.

I should be pleased to have written something. However, reading this piece deflates me. I have reduced a traumatic event, my own, to a mere 175 words. Moreover, this writing moment does not stimulate further writing. I set aside this experiment into nonfiction, wondering if I will be able to continue.

·······

Months have passed since I initiated this writing experiment. I willingly jumped down the rabbit hole of extensive preparation as a delay tactic. While delay is considered by some researchers on writing block to be an integral element of the writing process, allowing the writer time away to refresh, this usually takes place between drafts or between writing projects.[1] Time spent hesitating before the commencement stage of writing is often seen in those who are unprepared for the task at hand, be it through a lack of insider knowledge of how to write in the appropriate genre, or a lack of content knowledge.[2]

My reticence to attempt writing in this initial experiment is different: it stems from fear of failure. What if I cannot begin? What if the writer within is no longer there, that person who once had so much to say? What if my writing experiments are ineffective? Where will that leave me?

I attempt to address this fear with reasoning, using the analogy of 'riding a bicycle'. You know how people say, 'it's just like riding a bike - you never forget'? I simply need to start writing in any form as a way of climbing back on my bicycle.

While I remember the mechanics of riding, however, I have forgotten how to ride with ease. Mounting that bike after a decade away, I am hesitant, yet trust I will remember what to do. Once I start pedalling, however, my legs rebel. Did I even consider consulting them before embarking on this madness? My muscles scream, they burn and fail to respond the way I expected. It would be easy to give up. Go home, put away the bike for another couple of years. However, if I keep trying my bike, week after week, my muscles will start to remember. They will start to respond the way they used to. Soon, I will be riding along again, flying along, with freedom.

However, the mounting of this bike, my writing bike, is ineffective. My tyres are flat; I can go nowhere. I lift my eyes from those flat tyres to look outwards for support. I am seeking a writing model to follow, training wheels, an exemplar that I can mimic until I gain enough confidence to set out on my own.

With creative block set solid inside me, I constantly delay the moment of formulating a plan and proceeding to write. I make myself busy instead, burying myself in examining a new form revealed through my readings: the creative nonfiction essay. I delve into the book *You Can't Make this Stuff Up* by Lee Gutkind.[3] Perhaps attempting a creative nonfiction essay, instead of a feature story, is my way forward.

The personal essay

New to the creative nonfiction essay, I hope experimenting with this form might allow me to exercise both the intellectual side of the writing process, the one I am comfortable with, while potentially stimulating engagement in the creative side. From Gutkind's book, I learn that to appeal to a wider audience, to 'change minds and trigger dialogue',[4] my personal story needs to embrace a broader social issue.

My initial foray into this genre is to explore the notion of 'excuses'. There is much written about domestic violence in Australia, however, I find little written about why those who know, who see, who hear, do nothing.

As the basis of creative nonfiction is said to be scene,[5] I start with the following:

> There's a young couple standing outside a busy government office in a large country town in northern NSW. She could be 14, maybe 15; he looks much older, in his mid-20s. They're not related, that's obvious. He has chiselled features, full lips, olive skin and dark hair. His eyes are hidden by aviator glasses. Ray Bans. He's wearing expensive-looking, tailored clothes in a style reminiscent of the heroes of classic films. He reminds me of

Humphrey Bogart. But she's no leading lady. She has a round face, blue eyes, freckles and a blonde, curly bob. Her clothes are quirky, obviously hand made. He has an air of mockery about him, in the way he stands, the way he speaks to her. She seems unsure of herself, deferential to the man. They're arguing. She holds out her open, upturned hand towards him.

'Please give me my wallet,' she says. Her voice sounds so young, like a child's.

He steps in close to her, a gentle smile on his face. Looking her in the eyes, smiling sweetly, he punches and grinds the wallet into her lips.

Gagged, there can be no scream, just a muffled moan. He drops the wallet and walks quickly away.

Her face is flooded by tears; she is shaking so hard she can barely locate and pick up the wallet from the pavement. She stumbles, and still, not a sound. Her tears are silent, her gaze is down, away from the onlookers. Those who had been witness move on, resume their conversations, or begin speaking about what they have just seen. No one offers a kind word. No one offers assistance now that she is alone, which makes her feel even more alone. And worse, she will, at some stage, return to the room she shares with the man who just assaulted her, and pretend it never happened.

·······

While the fallibility of memory in memoir writing is of concern to many writers, the scene described above is imprinted on my memory, the intensity of the shock acting as a fast-closing lens. It has not been subject to changes ascribed to the telling and retelling of events, nor to 'the vagaries of time'.[6] I have not spent years dwelling on it. Writing this scene is the first time I have told what happened; it is fixed in my memory like a photograph in an album. Shelved, not thought about until the page is opened and the untouched image is revealed.

To situate my personal experience in a wider social context, I review information available on Australian Government websites.[7] It is distressing to read that:

- 1 in 6 Australian women over the age of 15 'have experienced physical and/or sexual abuse by a cohabiting partner'[8]
- There are 6,500 hospitalisations for injuries sustained in family and domestic violence every year, with First Nations people being over-represented[9]
- 'Women who experienced abuse during childhood were one and a half times more likely to experience violence in adulthood than those who had not experienced abuse during childhood'[10]
- 'Domestic violence has severe and persistent effects on physical and mental health.'[11]

Still, collating information and writing it into a coherent story are very different beasts. I cannot do it. After the short piece I wrote, I can write no more. I admit defeat with this genre. Regardless of the form, be it feature story or personal essay, I am unable to proceed. I decide to end this experiment into nonfiction and move on.

Not yet concluding

As I sit down to conclude this chapter, my news App opens a link to an Australian Broadcasting Corporation (ABC) feature claiming 'an inside look' into experience in a women's refuge in Brisbane.[12] I approach the stories with curiosity. What perspective does the journalist take? How would we, the readers, be called to action? Would these stories spark change in the way people think and act?

I doubt it. I cannot write a feature story, but I know how a good one reads. These stories are simplistic, superficially portraying people whose lives are far from simple. They read, and are even presented with colourful drawings, like a children's book. The tone is flippant and patronising; the writing full of cliches.
Consider the following sample:

> For someone who is a qualified professional and owns her own home, she must wonder how she has managed to find herself in such dire circumstances. Even so, Sally is matter-of-fact, even jovial at times. She's made a clean break and is getting on with the job of making her new life, even if it's a less-than-comfortable one.[13]

Can anyone honestly believe that a domestic violence victim who is in a women's shelter (after leaving the home she owned in fear for her life) is sitting about wondering how she magically ended up there? Even the words, 'managed to find herself' are designed to remove any external blame (such as on the perpetrator) and place it on the victim herself. And there is no way in hell she has made a 'clean break'.

I overflow with anger. Why are the real issues being ignored? Where is the discomfort? Where is the sense of outrage? Where are the personal links that connect me, the reader, to the people featured in the stories? It seems that domestic abuse is considered newsworthy, yet not important enough to be assigned talented journalists. This is a failed opportunity. Victims' stories need to reveal the complexity of their experiences. As readers, we can be called on to empathise with victims and survivors; encouraged to exercise compassion. I grow weary of hearing callous comments by people, including my highly educated female colleagues, that suggest a woman is in some way *deserving* of abuse because of her choices, or because of her childhood experiences. This 'othering' contributes to the systems that perpetuate abuse. It is in no way constructive.

I feel it intensely, this response to the failed opportunity of the ABC to use these stories to educate and create genuine discussion. Out of this intense frustration and anger flows the need to write. This is the result:

He has a way with words: an account of a 'domestic violence' survivor

'there is a high probability of violence when stalking persists for more than two weeks' [14]

There's another one in the mailbox. A handwritten letter, in a reused envelope with a long-past postmarked stamp. I take it to the police. This is the third item placed in my mailbox this week.

The uniformed officer at the counter is male. They're always male. White and male. His scowling face shows me what he thinks. I'm scum.

He throws the envelope down on the counter.

'It's a letter from years ago. Look at the stamp,' he grunts.

I take a deep breath, try to explain that he steals my rubbish.

I'm speaking words; he's hearing 'stupid female trying to

get some poor bloke into trouble'.

'Why don't you just throw it in the bin,' the officer tells me. He tells me, he's not asking.

I stutter, finding it incomprehensible: the need to go over and over the reasons. The same reasons. That he's been charged with rape, that there are bail conditions, and a protection order taken out by the police. That this is proof that he's been to my home again.

'Get a life,' the officer spits.

Scorn. He looks at me with scorn.

I want this all to stop. I want the stalking to stop.

I've been told previously by Police and by the Domestic Advocacy Service that I must report all breaches. I want to make a statement. I'm not leaving until I make a statement.

The officer refuses. I insist.

The officer changes tactics. He wants me out of there.

'If you don't leave, I'll have you charged.'

Another threat, and this time by the Police.

I burst into tears.

The officer and my partner exchange looks. I feel it, the embarrassment emanating from my partner. He takes hold of my upper arm, lifting me slightly out of my shoes.

I am shaking. I shake a lot these days. I am powerless to stop the stalker, as powerless as I was when he attacked me. I leave the police station, this latest incident of breach of bail conditions going unrecorded.

The next day, I chop down the tree that stands next to the mailbox, leaving nothing for a night stalker to hide behind. The act exhausts me but gives me hope. False hope. A few days later, after I find another hand delivered letter, I remove the mailbox entirely. The postie takes to tossing my mail onto the ground, but at least I no longer have 'mail' delivered at night.

But the stalking continues and expands into new avenues. When I visit my doctor, he tells me that the stalker has been to see him, to talk about me. When I go to my Spiritual Healer, the gentle soul who provides me with brief moments of respite, he tells me the stalker has been to see him, to talk about me. I attend an appointment with my psychologist who tells me the same story. I alert the head of security at the campus where I work, and they have a photograph of him, will keep a look out. But I have no 'look out' at home, and security camera systems have yet to become a common household item, the technology not yet advanced enough to reduce the price from thousands to only hundreds of dollars. I pay a private 'detective' to monitor my house for a few days, to take a picture of the stalker in action. I pay in advance, which is clearly a mistake, as I never see or hear from him again.

Unabated, the stalking continues. My electricity is turned off on 'special' occasions: my birthday, his birthday, the anniversary of the night he raped me, and Valentine's Day. I am too afraid to go outside to turn it back on. Instead, I draw the bolts on the inside of my bedroom door and hide until daylight, kept company by my dogs.

Section 359B of the *Queensland Criminal Code Act 1899* deals with stalking. It involves three criteria: intentional actions/behaviours, types of actions/behaviours and outcome. Simplified, they are as follows:

1) Intentional actions/behaviours include following, loitering, watching or approaching the 'stalked person'; and

2) Contact with the 'stalked person', be it directly through

mail, phone calls, emails and the like, or indirectly, through leaving items where they can be found by the victim, or invasion of the victim's visual and physical surroundings through the actions/behaviours mentioned in 1) above, or intimidation, threats or violence; and

3) These actions cause the 'stalked person' fear.

While an Act defines terms and states maximum penalties, it is up to the Police to first lay charges.

But the Police do not lay charges or follow up on most of my complaints. When they do follow one up, one, out of several dozen, they tell me it was a coincidence. He simply didn't know the people he'd been to see were my Doctor, Spiritual Healer and Psychologist. The officer speaks about his conversation with the stalker fondly, as if he's a dear friend.

Surely seeking out all three of my personal providers is more than coincidence? So again, I push.

I'm told it is not worth Police time to follow through with charges. How can the Police prove he intentionally visited my health care providers? I'm told a magistrate would throw it out of court.

For a brief time, there is the show of Police presence in my street. I see a marked car drive past, always in the early afternoon, not at night, once, twice, three times and then no more. When I contact the Detective in charge of the rape investigation, I do so out of desperation. This is the same Detective that told me no jury would believe me because of the inconsequential nature of my facial injuries. I take this step because there has been another parcel, one legitimately delivered by Australia Post, with my name and address handwritten by the attacker, stalker, rapist. He had become so brazen by two years of uninhibited stalking that he felt no need to disguise his actions. Finally, clear-cut evidence that he is in breach of bail conditions and of the protection orders.

But I hear nothing back.

When I follow up with the Detective, I learn that no charges have been laid. The Detective says he simply told the man to stop doing it. There is laughter in his voice, in his eyes, like my concerns are nothing but a joke.

I demand an answer. Why is he not being charged?

The Detective shrugs and says, 'He's a charmer. He has a way with words.'

Discussion

Is it true? Have I finally responded to my emotions through writing? Have I genuinely written because the story was spilling out of me? This urge-driven writing represents a breakthrough, a temporary reprieve of my complete creative writing block, a moment's taste of writing at-will. It feels liberating.

Conclusion

It is time to end this experiment and move on to the next. It would be too easy to continue my circuitous exploration of creative nonfiction, to battle with the essay form, to make further attempts at a feature story. However, this is not required. The goal of each writing experiment is to attempt to write in a genre and see where that leads me.

Sometimes, the difficulty in writing arises not from the topic, but the restrictions of the genre or form we are attempting.

Unwilling to change my topic, I changed my form. My exploration of the personal essay produced an attempt at writing; however, it felt artificial, disconnected from my inner voice. The urge-driven writing that followed is such a contrast, connecting, as it did, with my emotional responses. Without the writing experiment to start this process, I would not have written at all.

While I do feel some hope, it is cautious. I understand that my writing block is not resolved. The breach I made in the walls of that fortress sealed up the moment I completed the final piece. What remains is a glimmer of hope that I will, one day, freely draw on my creative written expression, my writing for the self, whenever, and however I want or need.

Extemporaneous writing (December 2015)

Three weeks have passed since I concluded the first chapter. As I drive home from work, I hear on the radio that two more Queensland women have died today at the hands of their partners.

No, that language is wrong. It diminishes blame.

I will rephrase that.

Two women in my home state were killed by their partners today. Two, in one day. I arrive home, sit down, and write. I include here the non-fiction essay I wrote because I was driven to.

My childhood, my training ground

I always thought of my childhood as being the same as everyone else's: waking up to the sound of kookaburras calling from their perches on the power lines; riding a hand-me-down bike to school, no helmet; smashing open macadamia nuts with an old brick - the trick to stop them rolling away is to trap them in a dent in the path. There were summer days in the neighbour's above ground pool, all walking in one direction to create a whirlpool, and long hours spent playing with the other kids in my street. In those days, friendships formed easily, based on nothing more than proximity. When alone, I would take books starring adventurous children up a tree, or to a hidden spot in the yard, and read, oblivious to everything else. I knew I would grow up to be an archaeologist, historian, and writer. I never imagined I would grow up to become a serial victim of domestic violence. What child could? And yet it was during childhood that I learnt the rules I would later come to play by: unspoken rules on how to empower someone to control me, on how to quash my own needs and desires. Rules dictating my duty to stay with an abusive partner because I'd made my bed and I should lie in it. Rules that prescribed how the abuse was my fault, and that I deserved it. Rules that made me question my values, my beliefs, my sanity.

Looking back on my childhood, I realise it was not the period of innocence I have pretended it to be. Sunday afternoons rolling in the long grass or on freshly mown lawn, playing in the waves at the beach, or swimming with friends at the public pool. It was much more than that. It was an apprenticeship for domestic violence.

When I was naughty, which, as an active and inquisitive child I seemed to be frequently, I was punished, as children are. My punishment for misdeeds was a beating.

'Go and get the brown belt,' my father would say.

Sometimes it would be the white one.

These weren't the smart, thin, black or tan dress belts he wore to work: these were thick, wide leather monsters with heavy metal buckles.

Durable.

I would beg to be spared, but never was. Why I persisted in asking is beyond me.

I always ran to retrieve the specified belt. They were kept in the same place, no matter where we were living at the time: on the rack inside of his closet door. Sometimes I was given the choice, allowed to select which belt to use.

I wonder what would have happened had I not returned with a belt, had instead run away? It never occurred to me. Always, I'd run back with the belt and hand it to Dad. He would do it up into a loop and flex it between his hands, the thick leather making a smacking sound that made me wail with fear.

Swphack. Wphack.

It was in my best interest to stop crying, though, or he'd 'really give me something to cry about'. Whatever that meant. Silently, I would wait as he flicked the belt between his hands. He would watch me watching the belt. Transfixed? Is that how I should describe it?

Swphack. Wphack.

'Come here,' Dad would say, and the whacking noise would continue, the sound of belt on little girl's bare legs.

Once I'd been dismissed, I'd run to my room, where I'd lie face down on my bed and quietly cry. After some time, Dad would come and talk to me, sitting on the edge of my bed, can of beer in hand, taking me into his confidence. His beery voice was kind, gentle. I knew he was only doing what was best for me. The beltings weren't that bad. What I got was nothing compared to what he'd received as a boy, to what I would have received had I'd been born a boy. Then, he'd have really flogged me.

Lucky I wasn't a boy. Should be grateful. I knew that. I understood that. And I was.

I'd give him a kiss.

'I love you, Dad.'

And all would be forgotten.

I didn't always get off so easily, though. Once, I'd been riding a motorbike, a dirt bike they're called, along the suburban footpath. My neighbours had brought it in from their hobby farm. Wobbling, the bike a lot bigger than my skinny 10-year-old frame could handle, I'd fallen into the street in front of our house.

Stupid thing to do.

I heard a squeal of tyres, saw a concerned driver through the windscreen. I was yanked from the tumbled bike by my wrist and hoisted through the air to the side door of our house. The one facing the neighbours who owned the motorbike.

'I thought you were dead,' rasped my dad as he unbuckled his belt.

As I swung about, hanging from my wrist, I caught a glimpse of his red face, then the face of the girl next door staring. I heard myself screaming as Dad flogged me until I fainted.

That girl never played with me again.

I wished she hadn't seen. I didn't want anyone to see. I loved my dad.

From this I learnt two things. One, that hurting someone

doesn't mean you don't love them. Two, that it's important to keep family matters private.

Dad wanted me to be clever, encouraging me to speak back to others, to never let them have the last word. He liked me telling him stories about how I said this or that to him or her. I was his 'mini-me', the son he never had. At home, though, it was Dad who always had the last word.

I would try to speak out, sometimes, against what I felt to be injustices. After all, Dad encouraged me to speak up for myself. I thought asking to open the car window, on our Sunday drive to the coast, was justified. But really, it wasn't. The air-conditioning was on. It was only a short, four-hour trip. The whole family, all five of us and the dog, in a car with closed windows, my nose running as my father chain smoked. He'd give me one of his man-sized handkerchiefs to blow my nose.

'Hangkies,' I'd call them. Still do. I remember how they were always perfectly ironed. Actually, handkerchiefs were the first items I was allowed to iron. Mine folded into triangles, Dad's into squares.

'You're a good girl,' Mum would tell me, as I tried to help with the many chores that seemed to drain her happiness.

I so wanted to see her happy. To hear her laugh. I'd clown around, sometimes, when it was just the two of us. Trying to make her laugh.

In the car, I made my point by fanning the smoke away from my face with my hand.

Such a smart-arse.

The 'backhander' was my rebuke. Alerted by the tone in his voice to the danger ahead, I dropped my hand and sank back into the seat, waiting for the blow. He kept his elbow poised in my face for several moments, adding to the tension. He could deliver an effective backhander while driving down a steep mountain road, pointing out the view, and smoking. Quite a skill.

And my mother, who I loved to bits, ignored my pleas for her support. She turned away, as she always did. She looked cranky. Sounded cranky.

'Leave me out of this.'

How could she not take Dad's side? What choice did she have?

I cried silently, not wanting to get the 'something to really cry about' I was reminded of. I pretended not to be crying, pretended to be looking out the window at the view, rousing myself just in time to act excited when Dad pointed out our first sight of the ocean.

'What kind of ice cream do you want, Stace, Stace, Stace?' Dad would ask, using the fun name he called me when he was happy.

'Liquorish,' I'd say enthusiastically, as if I hadn't just been hit in the face.

It was either that, or I wouldn't get an ice cream when we got there.

In this way, I became a great pretender. So ingrained was this duality, that I've only recently been able to recognise it.

My childhood was my training ground, and in my adult years I starred in my own rendition of this theme. Not that all the men in my life have been abusive, but I stayed with those who most manipulated me, most reduced me to an accepting, complacent child, the ones that were the most erratic in behaviour, and the most outwardly charming, and therein lay the danger.

Like many women who have suffered at the hands of violent men, I consider myself lucky to be alive. I've lost my savings, investments, superannuation, friends, jobs, my self-esteem and my health. I've been stalked, attacked and have endured humiliations that I have spoken about in detail only to police and to courtrooms of strangers, the humiliations compounded by the adversarial court process.

And still, life goes on. Every day is an opportunity to regain some of what I've lost through the violence, the manipulation, the mental and emotional abuse. The day I write this, in my home state of Queensland, two women were murdered by violent partners. And they're just the ones that have been mentioned in the media, the 'high-profile' deaths. There are others, if not today, then yesterday and tomorrow. I could have been such a statistic and was not. And for that, I am grateful.

Today, I'm friends with many people in my street, and in the streets surrounding my street, friendships forming out of proximity and shared smiles. I often sit in my backyard, reading books about adventurous women, ones who throw off the shackles of unsatisfactory lives to bravely live their dreams. It's wonderful in my yard, with the lorikeets in the trees, the smell of eucalyptus, and my dogs lying in the sun or nudging me for attention. I'm watching my macadamia nut tree grow. Self-seeded. There should be nuts in a few years. I have a fancy, bespoke macadamia nutcracker set aside in anticipation. No more smashing them open with bricks.

I may not be far in terms of distance from where I began, but I have miles of experience within me.

Reflections

At the early stage in my research recorded by this first chapter, the tiny 'i' that was me, the incomplete self, believed that nonfiction, particularly a reported piece, such as a feature article, would be easier to begin with than fiction. That 'i' felt safe writing from a distance, with a narrator external to the story. The contextualising narrative of this first chapter is an example of this distanced self, quoting authors, statistics, discussing genre, reviewing the actions of the person being discussed (that person being the little 'i' that was the creatively blocked me). That distanced approach to writing was possible, while drawing on imagination, as is required for fiction, was not.

That little 'i' attempted to write despite the hesitations and the fear of failure. This produced false starts before actual engagement in the writing process.

Those small attempts initiated the catalyst that was to occur years later. They allowed the diminished me to initiate the scraping back of the surface soil to reveal the potential of undisturbed earth. Once that little 'i' began writing, there was an imperceptible movement towards an enhanced ability, albeit miniscule, to engage in the practice of at-will writing. I had climbed back onto that bike; I had managed to wobble along for a couple of metres. The distance I had travelled, though small, was enough to result in a piece of extemporaneous writing.

I would like to say to the person I was at that time, 'Well done!' However, I know she would not have been convinced. The perspective of the participant is naturally different from that of the observer. Looking back at that early stage in this project is like looking at another person's work. It was done by me, the person I was at that time, not the present me, all these years later. And yet, I have not forgotten what it was like to live in that state of block, the emptiness, the lack of self-expression, those many years when I was a lesser me, a little 'i', living without my creativity, unable to harness the power of writing.

·····

My first venture into extemporaneous, needs-driven writing reveals more than a move towards my goal of reconnecting with an at-will writing practice. The story itself reveals a truth about domestic abuse that connects my experience with that of many others: that of trauma bonding.

> *You're small/young/powerless or have given up much to be with this person. You are reliant on your abuser for food/shelter/affection/money/your social position. The abuser is kind at times, and this is confusing. In these moments you experience the person you love, or the person that you should love, because they are all you have. You are locked in position, unable to see the wrongs committed as the eyes of others would, if they saw, but they don't see, because it's hidden, the brutalities, the destruction of your identity.*[1]

We live according to patterns, habits, rituals. We get out of the same side of the bed that we always do, we greet our loved ones in the same way we always do, we respond to annoyances in the same way we always do. We do these unconsciously, as ingrained actions and responses. If you look, you can find patterns in your relationships, and the roles you play within them. Relationship patterns are powerful because they become cemented to certain emotions, aligning with integral values we may be unaware of, with the way we see ourselves.

A trauma bond is such a pattern. Like many of our patterns, it is hard to see where it begins and ends. Like many of our patterns, it is difficult to see beyond, and difficult to break: where does a circle begin and end? Unlike many of our patterns, however, the emotional underpinnings of the trauma bond lie in the trauma we are unable to escape. A child is wholly dependent on her parent(s) for all of her needs. The way that child learns to behave, experience, see the world, see herself, is formed through that terrible bond. Like people who are only attracted to caring partners, the person brainwashed through living in a trauma bond will conversely seek out the patterns she is familiar with. This is absolutely unconscious.

When I read Nicole LePera's, *How to do the Work*,[2] I could barely tear myself away from its pages, so real, so touching on my own experience did I find her discussions. Until I arrived at the section on trauma bonding. Once I began to read about it, I felt a numbness set in. I closed the book and walked away. For days, I was unable to face this very personal truth. When I returned to the book, I read the section with trepidation. I experienced waves of nausea, a temperature, breathing difficulties, and a desire to do anything other than continue reading. The truth about oneself is confronting. But finally, I had some real answers as to why and how it was that I had repeatedly entered into, and stayed in, violent and abusive relationships. Why I turned away genuinely caring, devoted partners, for those others. I now understand why it is so difficult for other women I have known, and all those that I have not known, to 'just leave'. Perhaps if such an understanding was shared by everyone, then there would be greater support for those most in need. Perhaps.

CREATIVE NONFICTION

Writing as insight

CHAPTER 2 DRAMATIC MONOLOGUE

Experiment 2 (March - April 2016)
Extemporaneous writing
Reflections

This creative block is not limited to writing. The creative aspects of cooking, listening to classical music, upcycling and DIY projects have also fallen flat. I have lost so much of what I once enjoyed. Significantly, I cannot engage with fiction: not in films, not in books. How am I to base my writing attempts on models when I cannot read fiction? The worry taunts me, whispering in my ear as I scan the library shelves for something that will catch my eye. And something does. Not fiction at all, but a title that captures my interest because of its connection with my topic.

The book is *Fury – Women Write about Sex, Power and Violence*.[1] I turn the book over and over in my hands, astounded that it exists. This book is tangible evidence that women can write about their experiences and be published in a format freely available in a public library. I select stories resonating with my own, allowing these to affect me. In the past I would have written a short story, or several, and harnessed the strength of my emotions to create an outlet that was both cathartic and productive. But right here and now, I cannot: expressive writing is no longer natural to me.

Despite the force of my responses to these stories, writing

block rises before me: a formidable, featureless wall. I see no way through, can summon no ideas, no plan for a story, despite personal experience to draw on. Simply, significantly, I cannot connect with my will to write. I think of Virginia Woolf and ask, 'how am I to begin?'[2]

Having no drive to write is symptomatic of my experience of writing block. My way forward in this instance is to reduce the pressure to perform. I set myself a minor task: that of writing no more than a few words or phrases in response to the stories I read in *Fury*. I hope, by taking such a small step, I might then find myself taking more steps, to eventually continue on the path of my own accord.

My task is to note down experiences I was reminded of when reading the stories in *Fury*. Experiences in which I was powerless, contexts in which I had no agency, in which my voice was silenced. As I write, a particular incident rises to the surface: my experience **after** being the victim of a violent sexual crime.

I write only a few words. My emotions are intense, yet I am unable to move them into language. This inability to write away my responses and feelings amplifies them. I want to stop but do not. Must not.

Over several days, I add a word here and there, building on those initial few. These will go on to form the basis of a piece fighting to make itself heard. A piece that gives me a voice. That acts as a megaphone for my unspoken responses to those who wielded power over me. I realise that I need to create a spoken piece: not a short story, but a dramatic monologue.

The dramatic monologue is used to address a silent listener. While they can be poetic and literary, I want the form of an 'open mic', where the speaker has a live audience and is ready to stare

33

down hecklers. The dramatic monologue, unlike the internal monologue, requires an audience; it is designed to be heard. By using 'you', I challenge the imagined audience to take a side, to decide if they belong to those I am accusing or not.

Following the book of short stories that inspired me, fury is my theme. Finally, I will unburden myself of emotion that writing block has prevented me from releasing. I will let it spill forth through words on a page, words that demand to be spoken.

Dramatic monologue

To the police prosecutor who forgot I was her key witness, the one who yelled as I gave evidence, forcing me to still my words, to silence my voice, to you I say,

'No, YOU stop speaking now.'

Do you even understand your role here?

You're a girl-child imitating older, bigger, male barristers, far more experienced than you.

Have some courage and choose your own way.

Make the effort to be a good female barrister, not a second-rate copy of tragic players that could never succeed in jobs outside of this farce.

And stop fucking yelling at me, I'm the victim.

To the District Court Magistrate who bellowed at me, who threatened to impose a protection order against me, an order to protect the rapist from me, I say,

Old man, you, wielding power in this miniature courtroom, this doll house, here when others would be retired.

Look at me. I'm 48 kilos. Use your brain.

I. am. not. threatening.

Can you seriously entertain that I need to be legally restrained?

My solicitor tells you I am the victim of a violent sexual crime.

You ignore her.

You refuse to hear that the man in front of you, the one holding his hands over his face, the man making whimpering noises, has been charged with rape.

Are you incapable of seeing how you're being played? Can't you here the laughter of the man we call rapist, the one you call plaintiff?

Pathetic vestige of a cruel past, in this place where you have all the power. You ignore my solicitor and yell, yell, yell at me. Rage puckers your wrinkled face into a shrivelled scrotum. If this scene were shown in the outside world, you would be exposed for what you are: biased and backward.

District Court Magistrate, old white man in ill-fitting wig, yielding your power in this tiny room, sitting high as you look down upon me. Revel in your moment of power.

There is nothing to restrain you. Right here, you are all powerful.

But only here, in this tiny domain. Outside, you are nothing more than a faded, never-has-been.

What a ridiculous role you play.

You are an un-thing, a mechanism, and nothing more.

So, wield your power now, while you can, blame the victim, allow the rapist to laugh.

I walk out of this sordid place today. You remain.

To the people who have said to me, 'He's just doing his job' about the barrister who defended the rapist, I say,

'What a useless comment. Fuck off, and never speak to me again.'

It's Australia; we have the liberty to choose our jobs, we have options. He won't be executed if he refuses on moral grounds. He chooses to do the job.

Would you say the same thing about the barrister who helps to free your child's rapist/torturer/murderer? Would you then say, 'That's OK, he was just doing his job?'

Maybe you would. My neighbour said as much about the barrister defending Daniel Morcombe's murderer.

'It's not his fault,' she said.

'He has to pay his bills.'

The man who attempted to have a child's murderer released from jail is just a poor man working hard to pay his bills.

Is that what you think? Good people do bad jobs - they have no responsibility for the actions they take to achieve their goals? That would suggest there could be no war criminals.

Bullshit.

Try putting yourself in someone else's shoes. A simple, basic means of making an ethical decision.

But that would require you to think critically, wouldn't it?

So, I return to my initial response to your useless, thoughtless, uninvited comment on my painful experience.

'Fuck off, and never speak to me again.'

To the extraordinarily large number of people I have heard over the years pass the offhand remark about victims of abuse, 'Why doesn't she just leave?' To you all, I say,

Grow some humanity. You have no right to make such a callous, ignorant remark. May your glass houses grow flimsy with age, and shatter at the first sign of trouble.

Dickheads.

To the police officer at my local Police Station who told me, in front of my partner, 'to get a life' when we went there to report yet another incident of stalking by the man charged with rape. To that white male police officer I say,

You are a truly disgusting person. I hope life treats you accordingly.

To the man who attacked and raped me, who stalked me for years, who openly laughed at me every time he saw me going into or leaving court, to the filthy piece of shit that embezzled my savings, stole from my mortgage, sued me, and did everything his perverted mind could think up to try to destroy me, to that low life I say,

I'm still standing.

Discussion

Fury is more than anger; it suggests the unleashing of destructive forces. What I have written is destructive because it shatters the notion of 'paralysis by niceness'.[3] My monologue does not hold punches, it gives vent to emotion through profanities, it yells with spittle laced words at the progenitors of systems that perpetuate the abuse of female victims. While my piece is not akin to the releasing of the furies – there is no vengeance or retribution – it uses the release of pent-up force that fury suggests. And when that long repressed energy is released, the space it once occupied fills with something new, something fresh. This is a taste of the empowerment offered by a personal writing practice, of writing for the self.

This experiment has allowed me to express emotions too long locked away. Complete creative writing block has been my fury's jailor, and this experiment has been the means of its release. Using a form dramatic in tone and intended to be spoken, the dramatic monologue, I have been able to write something when I felt I could write nothing.

Extemporaneous writing (April 2016)

Silenced, ashamed

'**Silence!**' The defence barrister is panting, his entire upper body heaving with faked emotion; a deranged cockerel interrupted in coitus.

I am **silenced**. I feel guilty, **ashamed**. I glance up at the jury, their pale faces stare at me, open mouthed. How can ordinary, good people, be asked to hear the filth that is the theme of this drama? Let them go to their jobs, their homes, their personal concerns.

My mother always wished to be on the jury of a rape case.

'Cut their balls off,' she'd say of rapists, spitting the words out.

I'm not sure where the anger came from. I wonder, for a moment, if my mother would support me if she knew what had happened? My parents will wear my achievements with pride, but the failures, the abuse from men? My pleas for help?

'Ask someone else,' they always told me.

Who else to ask for help other than those closest to me? The **shame** felt when others enquire why my family aren't helping. Bury the **shame** in **silence**.

I am **silenced** by the police refusing to listen, for surely it couldn't have been rape, he's such a charming man the investigating Detective tells me, when he tries to persuade me to admit that I was lying.

'No jury will believe you,' he says. 'Other women have black eyes, broken bones.'

I carry my lack of obvious injury with **shame**. The police photographer captures my unblack-eyed face, does not take pictures of the injuries I do have. This, too, becomes my fault: a pin in my skin that the defence twists and turns, mocking my pain. My fault. My fault.

I am **silenced**, can no longer speak. The lump in my throat grows and deforms, and I take to wearing scarves, my look, my fashion statement. My **shame** is a goitre threatening to smother me completely, blocking my attempts to breathe. I no longer speak. I survive, nothing more. I am **silenced**.

Reflections

A word on agency and voice

When considering agency, I like to begin with the notion that individuals have the capacity, to some extent, 'to shape the circumstances in which they live'.[1] Take the life of a prostitute in nineteenth century Melbourne, for example.

> *I follow her closely as she navigates the bustle of Little Lygon St, this woman who is dressed as a lady. I mustn't lose sight of her; she is my escape from domestic servitude. I am to live and work in beautifully furnished rooms, drinking tea from Dresden porcelain, wearing the latest fashions, adorning myself with jewellery. And I will have men drinking from my shoe.*[2]

People can and do exert influence over their own lives. This influence is in relation to, and within the constraints of, their beliefs (in fate, religion, personal autonomy), abilities (thought processes, experience, education/training, physical and mental health) and contexts (family, communities, work, groups, society, the wider culture). Agency is more than free will, more than acts of resistance;[3] it is to act (or not act) within these parameters.

To have agency, however, is not necessarily to have 'voice'. In situations such as domestic abuse, victims often lack agency: they are unable to exert influence over their lives. This, in addition to being voiceless. This voicelessness refers not to a lack of trying to speak out, but of being ignored, drowned out, shut down, muted. This voicelessness is one of being silenced by others. The woman is silenced in her home, the victim silenced by the legal system.

This inability to be heard is the most disempowering of all. Our screams are described by witnesses and reported in the news as 'squeaks' and 'squeals',[4] as if we are mice or piglets. Or playing games. We are infantilised; denied adult authority.

Through the dramatic monologue, I spoke loudly of those injustices. This is where writing for the self acts as an agentic method. In the privacy of our writing, intense emotions can be safely expressed. In that writing moment, in that writing space, there is no stifling of voice.

······

Revisiting this chapter, I recognise this as my first piece of trauma writing. At the time, I understood that in writing through strong emotion, I had momentarily breached the fortress that was complete creative writing block. Learning about trauma writing per se occurred later in the project (see Chapter 7). Only then did I realise it had been one of the strategies I had relied on before the loss of my personal writing practice.

When writing the dramatic monologue, I was writing for myself. I knew my words would not reach those I address. The key to writing fundamentally for oneself is the emphasis on 'I'. What matters with a personal writing practice is 'that *I* have heard'.[5]

Rereading that piece, I continue to feel the satisfaction and empowerment I gained on having written it. The anger, frustration, and distress at some of the injustices had moved through me and into words. Finally, they had been 'voiced'.

This is the fundamental quality of writing for the self: it is a strategy for raising our voices, for setting out what we have to say, and, through seeing those words, we acknowledge ourselves as the most important audience of all. We thus affect our lives. We make change not to our circumstances, but to how we perceive ourselves within the restrictions imposed on us. This is to have agency.

> *'a lack of power in the domestic sphere is replicated and amplified when one enters the public arena'*[6]

I note, in my writing, the link between the loss of my personal writing practice, through which I enacted voice and agency, and the silencing of my voice in the legal arena that had become my life. I think about the needs of other women and children, those who do not belong to the dominant culture in our society. How do they navigate the many institutions that victims of domestic abuse are thrust into and against? How do they access useful information?

Language issues may be the first thought, but even for native speakers there are difficulties that stem from context, such as personality, life experience, or education. Sometimes we are blessed with helpful staff; at other times, they are cantankerous, withholding, or rude. Sometimes, they are misinformed. And then we become misinformed.

Potential difficulties originate from either side: the seeker of information, or the gatekeeper of that information. So too, can they stem from both sides. Assumptions based on cultural differences, socioeconomic factors, dis/ability, appearance, dress, age: all of these can compound the difficulties that become barriers to seeking, accessing, and navigating the institutions that are available. As a seeker, we may have certain expectations based on our past experiences. We may not grasp what we are told because the information, or the delivery, does not match with those expectations.

The barriers, hurdles and difficulties I faced in reporting violence, and in defending myself against ongoing abuse, were immense, despite being an insider in the culture in which I live. Despite being an articulate native speaker of English. Despite my high level of education. Despite my privileged socioeconomic background. Despite my proximity to the institutions I dealt with.

Cast the web wider into the many communities in Australia, including the rural and remote. Imagine the difficulties I experienced multiplied for those who do not share my advantages. For those isolated by remoteness, lack of connections, lack of information, language, disability. For those for whom leaving a relationship counters cultural norms. For those without access to money or transport. For those unwilling to leave their children, elderly relatives, or pets. For those who choose the known dangers over the possible alternatives (homelessness, poverty, marginalisation). Seeking assistance is most often, difficult.[7] The way out of abuse is not easy. It is not simple. Leaving, if it is possible, is often the beginning of more trauma.

THE WRITING PROJECT

Writing as voice

CHAPTER 3 YOUNG ADULT FICTION

Experiment 3 (September-November 2016)
Extemporaneous writing
Reflections

Do you have a favourite book? Child, teenager, adult, mine has always been *Alice's Adventures in Wonderland*.[1] Intellectually stimulating, creatively inspiring, and resplendent with fantastical suggestions on how to behave in an array of situations, the words, attitudes and actions of the key characters often punctuate my thoughts. I am particularly drawn to the clever use of grammatical possibilities to conjugate new forms of words. My favourite of Alice's expressions is 'curiouser and curiouser'. I believe adults are able to produce, and enjoy reading, works for younger readers because we maintain a link with our younger selves.

The traits of young adult fiction (YA) include the narrative voice of a young person, and universal themes, such as coming of age.[2] Preparing for a YA piece, I looked to what drew my younger self to reading. I loved reading YA versions of 'true' ghost stories, adventure, and fantasy. I enjoyed taking the ideas I read about and looking to find evidence of them in the world around me. In that way I created my own stories of sorts, even if they were not written down.

When reading, it was the elements of adventure and the

extraordinary that most appealed to my younger, curious mind: blending the everyday with myth or supernatural forces. For me, fantasy is about becoming lost in a similar yet differing world, one where the protagonist is challenged and in which she challenges those she comes across. There is change, both in the character and because of the character's intervention in this other world. Such an emphasis on change reflects the aim of this project to bring about a transformation in myself.

In keeping with my topic, this piece will incorporate aspects of domestic abuse. As a child I could escape the oppressive atmosphere at home in various ways. Getting out of the house, I could play with friends in the street or at their homes, ride my bike, or take a book and read somewhere out of sight. This differs from my experience as an adult, where the abuse overtook my daily life, affecting quotidian and major aspects alike. Consequently, for this story, I need to regard the abuse as a child would: occurring only within set contexts. I also need to consider that a young protagonist would have less life experience than I do. I wonder, however, how do I 'unknow' what I know?

There are also many choices to make regarding plot, setting, protagonist and intended audience, which will influence the choices I make in terms of other themes, and the language I use. There is, too, the issue of length. To write a novel takes time, and such an aim goes beyond the scope of this project. My choice then is to write a short story, or to write part of a novel, perhaps a few consecutive chapters.

I imagine my about-to-happen story in the same way I think about any book I have read in its entirety. That is, I know the ending. Consider *Looking for Alibrandi* by Melina Marchetta.[3] When I think about this book, I do so with far more complexity than when I approached the initial reading. I continue to share the protagonist's innocence and growing pains, acknowledge the shocks she experiences and understand the mistakes she makes, all while knowing how the novel ends. For me, the story is not limited to the words that form the text: I took to the reading and bring to my subsequent reflections on the novel, my own experience and experiences, such as attending a Catholic 'Ladies' College, going to church, meeting an Italian family for the first time when my family moved to Melbourne, the discomfort and thrill of attending school formals, the glorious dreams and hopes when visiting an old university campus, with its sandstone buildings and promise of scholarly rewards.

I bring this feeling to the writing I am about to attempt. The story is more than progress towards the next event. The main character is greater than her description, actions or thoughts made known to the reader. She has a history, and more importantly, a future that expands in directions not shown in the text. Consequently, I cannot approach the writing of this piece as a short story. Instead, I will approach my writing attempts as if I am writing a novel, with the freedom of spaciousness that a larger work offers.

As I interact with this genre, I am experiencing genuine creative stimulation that is both intellectual and emotional. I feel excited by the prospect of creating a fictional world for my protagonist, because I too will be entering this fictional world.

Not only do these new-found responses reveal a desire to write creatively, but also the ability to imagine ideas leading to creative writing. Desire to write, and by this, I mean being driven from within, and the ability to imagine, are two of the fundamental aspects of the creative writing process affected by block. Without these, the third, the ability to be involved in acts of creative writing, is either not possible or not sustainable.

Does this shift away from complete block signal an end to this project? The answer is no. Breaking through the block is part of the solution, but not the entire aim. My goal is to draw on writing as a strategy **as and when** it is needed. That is, to regain my personal writing practice. When I am writing in my everyday life, for myself, because I can, then the goal will have been achieved.

And yet, even in my life outside of this project, there has been progress. I recently responded to the loss of a loved one by pouring words onto a page: the first time in many years. The writing moment was short and intense, and once it had passed, I found myself again standing in front of a formidable stone wall of creative silence.

I cannot sustain a connection with my creative expressive self yet. But that momentary experience of writing for the self encourages me. Losing my personal writing practice has torn at my soul to such an extent that I have felt like a shadow of my former self. Now I see the fortress of complete block for what it really is: formidable, not impenetrable.

Returning to the writing experiment at hand, thinking about, designing, playing out in my mind the story that I am about to write, is truly being involved in the creative process. Will my attempts in this genre lead to further lifting of the heavy cloak that weighs down my soul? Will it open up my expressive airways, allowing me to inhale the pain, joys and frustrations of life and exhale my response in written form whenever needed, as I once could? That is what I am working towards.

The following is an excerpt from the larger, messier piece I wrote during this foray into YA.

Anna

It had been a beautiful trip: the lushly wooded mountains and pure looking water were reminiscent of Tasmania, but the scale and number of the mountains, cradling the fjord in a seemingly unending array, were beyond comparison. It felt surreal that people could live in such a wild place. Houses, few as they were, appeared to cling precariously to their tiny plots of land on which it seemed as if the forest was encroaching. There were occasional tiny hamlets; houses grouped together at the water's edge with an army of trees bearing down on them. The houses were brightly coloured, unmissable amongst the almost solid wall of green. Like decorations on a Christmas tree. And then there were the tiny, tiny islands, not much bigger than Anna's backyard at home. These had one, two or three houses at the most. All had piers and boats.

Home. Anna raised her chin and tipped her head back a little. By keeping her head up high, she was able to hold off the choking sensation that came when her throat began to close up. But she couldn't hold back the tears. She moved almost blindly to the edge of the boat and faced the direction they had come from. She couldn't see the boat's wake, she couldn't see at all through the tears, but she knew it was there – a road without foundation, a path that cannot be trod on, a marker of the long distance travelled away from home. Anna felt sure no one would see her crying. The wind was strong here and most of the other passengers were sheltering indoors.

Anna tilted her head back even more, worried that if she allowed her head to dip towards her chest, she would crumple into a heap.

THE WRITING PROJECT

Home. Mum.

Anna was tired of being brave. She was about to give in to her grief when the ship let out a piercing whistle and the engines cut back. Anna looked around with suddenly seeing eyes and noticed they were amongst other boats. They were in a harbour, a small harbour filled with tiny boats, and it was her stop.

Using the knuckles of her index fingers, Anna swiped away the tears that hung over her eyes like mini curtains made of rain droplets, then moved quickly inside. She joined the crowd moving down the internal stairs, trying not to take the shoving personally. She located her wheeled bag and tugged at it until it finally moved. She joined the crowd again, this time moving towards the plank to go ashore.

...

Anna hung back and waited until most people had alighted. She was in no hurry. It was beautiful, with the coloured buildings overhung by masses of pine trees that lined the mountain behind. As Anna walked along the pier, people smiled and greeted her. So many people that she was starting to wonder if she was an innocent player in a joke. One particularly cheerful woman stopped Anna by grabbing her shoulders, drawing her close in a warm, soft, grandmotherly embrace, then holding her in such a way that her face was close to Anna's.

'Welcome home,' she said, her eyes twinkling.

And then she was past, and Anna continued moving along, confused by what had just happened but grinning from ear to ear with pleasure.

Crazy, Anna thought. She's just mistaken me for someone

else.

But she felt happy all the same.

Only then did Anna realise she could understand the voices around her.

They must all speak English, she thought. Lucky for me.

After asking for directions, Anna made her way to the local accommodation house.

'Hello,' she said, adjusting her heavy bag on her shoulder. 'I'm…'

'Anna,' the clerk said before Anna could finish.

'Yes,' Anna replied.

Of course, he knew who she was, Anna thought. There didn't seem to be any other guests arriving on the boat.

'I'm afraid there is no room available,' he said.

Anna gasped.

'But I've come all this way,' she began.

The kindly reception clerk stopped Anna before she grew too upset.

'Don't worry,' he told her. 'Family are going to host you.'

'Family?' Anna whispered. Did he mean his family? A family? What family? It seemed as if he was suggesting Anna's family.

'Look,' he said, interrupting her thoughts. He indicated over Anna's shoulder. 'Someone's here to collect you now.'

Anna turned but was unable to see clearly as the light from the doorway was eclipsed by a bear of a man.

'He must be at least two metres tall,' Anna thought, as his head obscured the lintel over the door frame.

Suddenly, the air was being squeezed out of Anna's chest. She couldn't inhale, her face crushed against the soft cotton shirt front of what felt like a chest of steal. Anna felt heady, short of breath. Her senses were consumed by a crisp, fresh smell of pine needles and wood smoke.

Bear man pulled back and lowered his face to hers.

'Welcome, little one,' he said in a voice as deep and rich as the gloss on the mahogany cabinet Anna's mum inherited from her parents.

'I'm Sune. We've been expecting you.'

He stood up, reaching for Anna's case and bag.

Anna stood still, feeling far too confused to react.

'Well, come on then,' he called back over his shoulder. 'There are people waiting to meet you.'

Anna followed him out of the building and along the street. They walked out of the central area, heading along a path that wound along the water's edge, then turned inland. They walked uphill for only a few moments, stopping at a house set in a small clearing.

'Here we are,' Sune said, turning his huge smile on Anna before flinging open the door.

Anna took a quick look around her before following him inside.

The smell of cooking welcomed her even before the people. Sune put her case down in the entry and stood to the side of a set of large double doors. He smiled at the room's occupants and announced, 'Here she is.'

Sune stood back and waited for Anna to approach the doorway. He must have realised her hesitancy, as he raised his bushy eyebrows in a dramatic gesture, slightly tilting his head to the left.

'Come on in, Anna, and meet the family.'

Anna walked through the doorway and there, facing her, was a room of people. They were smiling at her with the whole of their faces, their eyes glowing with warmth. She found herself being embraced, warm arms and chests, the soft touch of hair against her cheeks, the scent of each person momentarily enveloping her. Anna was swept up and into a chair, a hot drink placed in her hands. The people were spread out in a crescent before her, leaning forward, with Anna as centre of attention.

Anna sipped the spiced drink, feeling its vitality spread through her throat, chest and belly. She answered their questions about her trip and must have yawned, as the mother announced that she was to be shown to her room.

'Take a nap and we'll call you when it's time for dinner,' she said, her face and tone so gentle, so kind.

Anna stood and followed the child charged with taking her to her room. As she passed through the hallway leading to the staircase, she noticed a painting on the wall and her heart plummeted into her stomach. She knew that scene. She used to have a dream. She was there, in that place, the one in the painting, and there was no movement, no sound. It was like being in a vacuum.

Anna could feel a presence near her and realised that one of the daughters, Keri, the one the same age as Anna, was next to her, also looking at the painting.

'The place of everything and nothing,' she said.

She spoke, but so did Anna: they were speaking the same words at the same time. Anna stopped. Keri stopped.

'I was terrified,' Anna said, but as she said this, Keri's mouth formed the same words.

Anna stood still, entranced. Keri hadn't moved and yet she was no longer next to Anna but standing face to face with her. Keri turned away, looking back at the living room, the sounds of happy chatter reaching out to them.

'We all have that dream,' she said, then turned back to face Anna.

'Rrrraaagh,' cried the youngest sister, Mani, running out of the living room and crashing into their legs.

'I'm a lion, I'm a LION. Rrrraaagh.'

Anna laughed. Keri laughed. The spell broken, they climbed the stairs to Anna's room, pretending to be escaping the ferocious lion.

Anna fell asleep in an instant. It seemed only a moment later that Mani was sitting on her bed, bouncing her plump little body restlessly to wake her up.

'Anna, ANNA,' she repeated.

Laughing, Anna got up and together they followed the delicious scents downstairs to the living room. A smaller number of people were there this time, members of the immediate family. Anna was hugged by each one in turn.

Every person she embraced smelt delicious, like so many joyous scents: the children like spice cookies or toffee apple or vanilla ice cream; the women like orchids, rainforests or summer evenings near the beach; the men, like pine needles, sandalwood and roasted chestnuts.

'Come on through to the dining room,' Lilia, the mother, invited, and Anna took the seat proffered her.

The table was covered with delicious looking dishes; the centrepiece, a large joint of roast meat.

Anna immediately thought of her mum. She had taught

Anna how to behave in such a situation.

'Be polite but firm,' she'd said, watching Anna closely, her eyebrows raised, head slightly tilted.

She'd wanted to see that Anna had really understood: their beliefs, her beliefs, were important to her mum.

Still, Anna had only just arrived in the home of these amazingly hospitable people. They'd opened their home to a stranger and now she was about to reject the highlight of their meal.

Anna's chest raised high and filled out as she took a deep breath of courage. She was just turning to Lilia to speak when she was passed a plate piled with a range of vegetables and a slice of meat.

'We know you're a vegetarian, so we're just offering you a taste. It's venison.'

Anna gasped.

'Venison. That's deer, isn't it?'

'It is,' Lilia said with a firm nod of her head.

Lilia looked over at Sune.

'Anna,' said Sune. 'This is from an old male that had a long life. He recently lost his group to a young usurper. He was suffering from serious injuries from their battle. He had a long life and produced many, many offspring. We liberated him from a lonely, drawn-out death.'

Lilia spoke next.

'It was so fast, Anna, he didn't even know we were there until the shot was fired. Sune held his hand gently on the steer's heart until it stopped beating.'

'We don't eat cruelty,' Sune added. 'The animals and us, we live as one.'

Anna took a breath and, picking up her knife and fork, cut a slither off the thin slice of meat on her plate. She placed it in her mouth.

Anna blinked, and the meal was over. She was full and felt slightly intoxicated. The table had been loaded with food but was now empty. She didn't remember eating the meal. She tried to stand but her head was spinning. There was a hand at her elbow.

'Let me help you,' a gentle voice said, and Anna inhaled a deep, rich scent that made her feel calm and safe. Anna was led to a seat by the window in the living room.

'What do you miss about your home?' someone asked.

Anna inhaled deeply and closed her eyes. She was in her backyard. The afternoon sun was reflecting off the ghost gums. She was watching her dogs playing their goofy games: Jack digging up the lawn, Molly almost laughing with glee as she rolled in the dirt. She noticed the colours of the leaves and the tiny flowers of the native plants, the high, high blue skies and cotton ball clouds.

'Everything,' Anna replied. 'Everything.'

'I miss the sound of the rain on the tin roof, the way the tree branches droop heavily and the birds in the trees still sing despite the downpour; the way my ducks revel in the temporary ponds in the backyard, happily sieving the mud through their beaks. I miss my dogs and my friends. I have a community there. Had.'

'And now you have us.'

Anna looked up and all eyes were on her. She felt immersed in warmth. And something else. It felt like a strong sense of anticipation.

Anna realised she was holding her breath. And so was everyone else.

'Greetings,' came happy voices from the doorway. Within moments, visitors had taken places among them. The room brimmed with chatter, laughter and the sound of glasses chinking.

That night Anna dreamt she was in a forest clearing and she could see a family of deer grazing. They seemed peaceful. There was a sudden movement and Anna froze with fear. A creature, a changeling, part man part animal, was at the edge of the clearing. It was holding the youngest deer. Anna turned and ran and ran, and it wasn't until she stopped running that she realised that she, too, was a deer and that she had been running for her life. Anna was exhausted and near to collapse. She bent down to drink from a puddle and saw, reflected in the water, the face of a man behind her. It was Sune.

...

In the morning Anna sat for a while in bed looking at pictures of her mum, their home, and the life that was gone forever.

Anna's mum was always smiling. Well, nearly always, except when she was fighting with her dad, which happened a lot, but that all stopped when he left. And now her mum's gone, too.

Since her mum died, Anna's life felt meaningless. Every simple, daily act felt mechanical. Slow and mechanical. And difficult.

There were neighbours, parents of friends, her mum's friends. People all around, but Anna's world was empty. Days slipped by and she seemed to be fading. The principal of her school called her in to her office one day and asked how she was coping.

'I'm not,' Anna said. She thought, why pretend to be what I'm not?

Anna and Sister sat in comfy armchairs, at a long antique coffee table. Anna loved those chairs; they made her feel cosy and embraced. Safe. Sister's assistant brought them in a tea tray, and there they sat, Sister Mary Ann and Anna, drinking tea. China teacups and saucers. Silver sugar spoon. She offered Anna a scone. Cream, jam. Anna used to love scones. She sighed, took one and tried to eat, but the fluffy scone turned to glue in her mouth, and she couldn't swallow. Anna's eyes welled with tears. She stifled a sob as she spat the lump into a tissue.

In a gentle voice, Sister Mary Ann asked Anna to go over to the mantel piece to get a framed photo for her. Anna did as she asked, and as she lifted the frame, she noticed herself in the huge mirror hanging above the fireplace. She looked thin, pale, with dark smudges under her eyes. And her eyes were sunken. Smaller, somehow. Anna then noticed in the reflection that Sister was watching her, with concern in her expression.

'Bring the picture over here, Anna dear,' she said, and Anna took it back to her seat.

'See this picture?' Sister Mary Ann asked. 'See that lovely face there? That's your mother when she was almost the same age as you are now.'

For a moment Anna forgot everything else as she gazed in wonder at the small image of the face of her mother long before she was a mother. When she still had her life before her. Sister added something which Anna had only just realised herself.

'You look just like her.'

Anna started to cry. 'I'm all alone, Sister. I want my family.'

'I know, dear.' She said, putting a soft, warm arm around Anna's shoulders. 'I know.'

Through the kindness and generosity of many people, Anna's school arranged for her to spend a year in the country her mother was from.

...

It was Anna's second night in Norway. The summer days were so long, Anna just knew she wouldn't be able to sleep. She decided to go for a walk.

As she wandered the streets, Anna felt as though she was catching a glimpse into the intimate part of the lives of the town's inhabitants. She's laughing at a TV program at this house; he and she are seated on a comfy sofa, leaning in close as they listen to a piece of beautiful classical music; children are laughing and running in this house, the sound of their little steps followed by the heavier ones of their father, who is making deep monster noises which sends them into squeals of delight; then silence as Anna approached a house with no life inside at all.

Perhaps the residents are out to dinner, she thought.

As she passed the house, Anna heard a crash from inside, and turned to notice a light in one of the upstairs rooms. A deep voice bellowed, 'Happy now?'

There was no answer before the next bellow.

'Answer me!'

There was another crash, louder this time. It sounded

like furniture being pushed over. And there was a scream. A woman's scream.

'Stop it. Please,' begged a woman's voice.

Anna's heart plunged into her stomach and her ears began to roar. She turned and ran back to where she was staying.

That night Anna dreamt of when she was a child. Instead of being asleep in bed, she'd crept part way down the stairs to listen to the TV. Mum liked to sit up late and watch TV once the chores were done, and Anna was in bed. That night, it wasn't the TV Anna could hear, though, but the voices of her parents. They were arguing. Her dad sounded angry. His voice was strange, like it was when he'd been drinking beer. Her mum sounded upset. Anna couldn't understand what they were talking about. Perhaps she was too young. But there was yelling, and a large crash, and her mum screamed, 'Stop it, stop it!'

Then there was a strange sound, like a smack on bare skin, and her mum was crying.

'You're worthless,' Anna's dad had yelled as he left the room. He walked past Anna and out the front door.

He didn't see her.

Anna heard the car engine roar, then the car speeding down the driveway.

Quietly, Anna inched her bottom down the rest of the stairs, one at a time. She crawled along the floor to the lounge room and peered around the door frame. Her mum was kneeling on the floor next to her antique display stand, the one Anna was always told to keep away from. Look but don't touch. Everything was on the floor, and her mum's favourite picture of grandma, grandpa and her, the one in the guilt frame, was broken. She was holding the picture, but it was in two pieces. Her face was blotchy looking, and swollen on one side, and her hair was messy.

'Mum.'

She looked up and Anna saw her face change. Her eyebrows wrinkled in towards each other, and the middle of her lips seemed to suck into her mouth. Then she breathed deeply and sighed.

'Oh, darling,' she whispered. 'Let me take you back to bed.'

The next morning, Anna ran into the lounge room to see if the antique display stand was still broken, but it wasn't. It was standing where it usually stood, but somehow it looked different. When she looked at it closely, she realised many of the special objects that so fascinated her, most likely because she wasn't allowed to play with them, were gone. She wanted to ask her mum where they were, but when Anna saw her face, she decided not to. Her mum had a cold. Her eyes were puffy, one cheek was bigger than the other, and one eye was partly closed.

'Run out in the garden and play with Jasper,' she told Anna.

Anna did. She played and played and played with Jasper until he was too tired to chase the stick and lay in a panting heap on the ground. She went over to him, lifted his soft, furry ear and whispered.

'Mum's been crying. Dad hit her.'

Jasper panted heavier as if he understood the implications. Then Anna saw her mum was watching them. She looked even sadder. Anna pretended she hadn't seen her, and pressed her face into Jasper's fur, cuddling and kissing him. When she looked up again, her mum had gone inside. Anna could hear her crying. She cried for a long time, and then there was silence. When her mum came out to get them, she was smiling again.

'Guess what I've made, Anna?' she asked.

'Pikelets?' Anna squealed, glad to see her mum happy again.

'Even better,' her mum said, bending down to hug Anna as she ran up to her.

'Chocolate chip cookies!' she announced, and Anna jumped up and down in excitement.

'Chocolate chip cookies!' she yelled. 'Chocolate chip cookies, Jasper.'

Jasper, aroused by her excited tone, leapt up on Anna and her mum. When Anna laughed, her mum did, too. Anna just knew that everything was all right. That everything would be fine.

'Well, they're ready to eat,' her mum had urged. As if she needed any encouragement! Anna had a plate of chocolate chip cookies and a glass of milk, just like she'd seen on Sesame Street.

...

Home-made biscuits. The smell was unmistakable. Anna lay in bed, luxuriously inhaling the smell.

How could a dream be so real? she wondered.

There was a knock. Anna opened her eyes to see Mani peering around the door.

'Mamma made biscuits!' she almost squealed as she jumped onto the bed, landing on Anna's legs.

'Biscuits. For breakfast!' she emphasised, her large blue eyes almost popping out of her head.

The smell was real. Biscuits. Anna could smell the vanilla,

almost taste the butter on her tongue. She drew the scent deeply into her lungs.

'Well,' interrupted Mani, 'Aren't you going to get up?'

Anna looked at Mani's face. She looked quite serious.

'Well, aren't you?'

'Actually, I thought I might spend the day in bed,' Anna said casually, turning away her gaze and donning a look of nonchalance.

'But they're for you,' cried Mani, becoming distraught. 'Mamma says we can't have any until you come down!'

Mani's face started to crumple, and Anna caved.

'Well, I'd better get up then,' she said, extricating herself from Mani's weight and slipping out from under the covers.

'Biscuits for breakfast it is,' Anna said, as she grabbed her robe and turned towards the door.

After their very special breakfast, Anna returned to her room to dress. She couldn't stop thinking about the dream she'd had. Anna hadn't remembered that night before. She supposed she'd put it all out of her mind. It had been nice living with just her mum and Jasper, then Jack and Molly. And yet she had missed her dad. She had missed him reading to her at night, not always, but sometimes, when he hadn't had too many beers. And she had missed his jokes and silly sayings.

Discussion

While the fantasy element is not so evident in the sample above, I included more in the longer piece. As my writing progressed, I found myself wondering if the fantasy aspect was necessary. I felt I was trying to include too many elements in one story. However, in allowing myself to play with fantasy, I gained a greater sense of freedom when writing. I gave myself permission to write ideas as they arose. This generated segments that may not fit into the story, or that need to be held aside until a suitable place arises. Or else, it meant a scene I wrote could lead to various possibilities, depending on how I might like to run with the fantasy element. Through embracing fantasy and following the White Rabbit whenever he materialised, I have experienced deep engagement in creative thinking and writing.

Extemporaneous writing (September–October 2016)

While working on the YA chapter, I found myself wanting to write more.

Ah ha, I thought. The desire to write!

Curiously, as I drafted the following piece, I became aware of certain traits finding their way into my writing. These include repeated actions, events, behaviours and phrases. Perhaps these elements identify my writing as my own: little sprays of scent across each piece, the smell of me. Or perhaps they are stuck points, elements demanding attention through writing until they dissipate. I began with a scene from my adult life in mind, approaching this nonfiction piece as a short story.

YOUNG ADULT FICTION

short story, draft - The adult has grown from the child

The wardrobe is smaller than I remember a wardrobe to be.

It is dark, cramped and smells of nothing in particular, the place is a new-build after all, and we're the first tenants.

I sit here, my knees drawn up to my chest, holding my breath, ears attuned to every sound outside my dark, cramped space.

When I was little, the wardrobe in the room I shared with my little sister was capacious.

There were no shelves; just a long rail across the top, well out of my reach. Clothes hung there would soon make their way down to the pile below, happy to be amongst friends.

Clean up your room! I'd be told, meaning, get out of here, we're arguing, we don't want you there gawping at us.

I'd open the wardrobe and push all of my toys, clothes, school bag and books inside, attempting to close the door before it all came crashing out.

I think of those contents now, spilling out on the floor, like guts and brains from a mangled carcass.

Once I'd hid in there to read. I'd found a torch, who knows where I got it from, dad wasn't handy nor a 'prepare for storms' sort of man, and pretended I was in the adventures I was reading.

The door was pulled open by the scoffing older sister. She yelled out, projecting her voice outside the room into the rest of the house,

Stacey's doing something dirty in the wardrobe.

No, I'm not, I whined, but it wasn't the truth she wanted to hear. She didn't want to hear anything from me at all. She was just there to be mean. But I got her back, told on her for smoking. I may have received a belting for telling tales. Maybe, maybe not: so many beltings, some are hard to tell from another.

I hear footfalls in the corridor: he's home. He's not big like my dad was when I was little, but he's the boss of me all the same. He's a lot older, he's French and I'm a dirty little Antipodean, offspring of a bastard culture. Not that we have any culture in Australia, he tells me, and I believe him, as I believe everything he says.

......

It feels liberating to be able to write just because I want to. I returned to this story the following day, passionate about reworking it, improving it, making it more of a skilled piece of writing. I wanted to emphasise the notion that in domestic abuse, the child's lived experience becomes that of the young adult. Over the subsequent days, I reworked this story into new versions, each time focussing on different aspects. Each version grew in length. Ten days later I concluded with my fifth version. While comparing and contrasting them would make a useful exercise in a writing classroom, I will not subject you, dear reader, to all of these versions. Instead, I provide a table overviewing key differences, revealing the thought process that led from the initial to the final piece.

DATE	WORDS	PERSON	FOCUS	CHANGES
original 24 Sept	374	first	getting story down	
rewrite 25-26 Sept	591	first	adding detail	increased sense of being trapped
rewrite 27 Sept	668	first	more description	increased contrast childish dreams and family dysfuntion
rewrite 29 Sept	808	first	increased detail/sense of fear	changed protagonist's name
rewite 1-3 Oct	960	third	focus on narrative	external narrator introduced, more visuals

In shifting from first to third person, I expected to gain distance from the story. This does not happen. In fact, I feel even closer to the protagonist. Perhaps this is owing to the insider information provided by a narrator who knows everything about the protagonist's life – her past, her thoughts, her fears. So, despite trying to remove myself from the story, I am there all the same, as the narrator who knows it all. To make this notion a little trickier, lines like 'shhhh' are not allocated to the character, so they may belong to the narrator or perhaps even an unmentioned observer. This is a choice to be made by the reader.

final version 1 – 3 Oct

The walls are pressing against her. They feel so flimsy that she's afraid her restless elbow, the right one, will poke a hole through into the corridor. She can hear her own breathing and she looks up, creating more space in her chest and throat to release the tightness. She immediately wishes she hadn't; she's noticed the shelf above her moving closer.

Calm. Remain calm.

How the hell can I remain calm when my pulse is exploding out my ears?

Shhhh.

Wardrobes used to be bigger.

She blames the cheap and nasty new build. Crappy brick veneer duplex in a cheap and nasty housing estate is what he calls it.

He mocks the tiny streets, the tiny dwellings, the togetherness of it all, and particularly the residents. She does, too. Peasants.

She hugs her knees to her chest.

God, this is uncomfortable.

Too late to find another place now. Nowhere else to go, not without explaining to the friend whose door would open in welcome, if only she were to ask.

But she doesn't ask.

Her belt buckle is digging into her stomach. Bile is rising and she needs some water: just one cool sip would suffice.

Why did I drink, why did I drink? I speak too much when I drink.

She must have been holding her breath. Her chest is burning in the way it did when she completed her swimming safety certificates at school. But hold her breath she will. There's no way she's going to be one of those people who get eaten by monsters in movies, the ones who sneeze, or exhale at just the wrong moment. Quiet, she must be quiet, must listen, but how can she be quiet when the cramped space amplifies every minute sound?

The wardrobe in the room she long ago shared with her younger sister was cavernous. There were no shelves, just a long rail across the top, well out of her reach. Unless she jumped up and grabbed for it, which was fun. The hanging clothes fell onto the pile below and out onto the floor of the room.

'Clean up your room!' they'd yell at her, her parents, meaning, get out of our sight, we're arguing, we don't want you gawping at us, with your fat round face and your thin scraggly hair.

In that room, she'd open the wardrobe and push all of her toys, clothes, school bag and books inside, trying to shove the door closed before it all came crashing out.

She pictures those contents spilling onto the floor: guts and brains cascading from a rotting carcass.

Once she'd hidden in the wardrobe to read. She thought reading in the dark would be fun. There was nothing but her and the book, a birthday present from a friend. Away from the tension that hung like insecticide in the living areas of the house, she could be part of the adventure, one of the characters, solving the mystery, knowing that they'd get the bad guy, that …

The door was pulled open and the other sister, the much older one, was there, upper lip curled in a hideous sneer.

'Roxy's reading something dirty,' she bleated loudly.

She'd stopped breathing then, too. And there was ball of something stuck in her throat, a lump of dough like when she'd eat a thin slice of the hot cheesy-smelling bread her dad would get from the Hot Bread Kitchen on the rare Sundays they'd visit her Gramps.

'You're a dirty little pervert,' croaked the older sister, the one she hated so much.

'No, I'm not,' Roxy whined. Whine, whine. Whinger, the older sister used to call her. Among other names. She was so mean.

The loud steps she'd been dreading stopped in front of her. She was wrenched from the space by one arm and dragged into the lounge room. She stood still, very still, for her interrogation. She could see the older sister in the corridor, watching, round face cracked in a smirk.

But she'd get her back, not then, but later. Would tell on her for smoking.

'Don't tell tales,' she was told. The belting was to make the point clear. Did the older sister get into trouble? She doesn't know. She'd been lying face down on her bed crying, the backs of her legs burning in belt-width welts.

Here, now, she hears footfalls in the corridor. He's home. He's not big like her dad was when she was a little girl, but he's the boss of her all the same. He's so much older, he's French, so sophisticated, and she's a dirty little Antipodean, offspring of a bastard culture.

Not that Australians have any culture, he always tells her.

Australians don't have any culture, she says to people, knowledgeably.

He stomps down the tiny corridor in that doll-house sized duplex. He goes straight to the room and wrenches open the wardrobe's sliding door. Almost pulls it off its tracks.

He looks at her, eyes mocking, pointy nose raised on one side in a sneer, distaste dripping from the lips she finds so sensuous.

Out she's dragged by the hair. She stands and takes the beating, the one she deserves for humiliating him by not dressing as smart as she should have at the function earlier tonight, for not being able to engage in sophisticated conversation. He whacks her across the head. You're totally lacking in culture, she's told. Peasant.

From then onwards, the wardrobe remains open. Her clothes stay on the floor, and he walks on them, making a show of grinding them underfoot. She sees him do it and wants to move them out of the way, to fold them or place them on hangers. But she doesn't. Instead, she walks on them, too.

······

Discussion

I have enjoyed this unplanned writing adventure, writing spontaneously, then reworking this story; answering the call to write in the midst of exploring YA fiction. Significantly, there **was** that call to write. Desire, and responding to the desire to write, is what complete creative writing block took away from me. This foray into writing beyond the structure of my experiment suggests I am moving away from complete block.

Reflections

Rereading this chapter on YA fiction, I am reminded of what is referred to as 'resilience' in children who experience adversity. As a child, then later as an adult, I employed what is known as 'avoidant coping strategies'[1] for dealing with the shame and fear resulting from my abusive home life. These strategies do not address the abuse. Instead, they shield us from thinking about the abuse.

As a child, I found distraction in play, sport, music, reading, and occasionally, television. As an adult, I continued to smother thoughts of the abuse through exercise, study, and work. Research has found links between the use of avoidant coping strategies and later development of greater symptoms of post-traumatic stress disorder.[2] In this, unresolved stressors from childhood compound with later stressors. Positive coping strategies, such as drawing on social support at the time of traumatic events, however, have been found to lessen the impact of trauma. This means dealing with our emotions regarding the abuse in a timely manner. Writing for the self can be one of these positive strategies.

I have returned to the fuller piece that I wrote, then reduced, for the above YA piece. I include here an excerpt from that fuller piece out of wonder at my own resilience as a child. Much of the piece included above was fiction; the following segment, not included in that final piece, draws on my lived experience.

> Anna's dad was so angry that night. Anna and her mum knew it from the slam of the door and the noisy stomping of his feet. Her mum jumped up from the table and began crashing dishes and cutlery in the sink.

Anna continued to sit at the table. She couldn't leave until she had eaten everything on her plate. She tried to cram the cold grey balls of cabbagey-things into her mouth, but her stomach was twisted in a knot.

Just inches from her chair, her dad stood, bawling and braying at her mum's back. On and on.

Anna felt a whack on the back of her chair, and stopped eating, fork in hand.

'And stop mollycoddling her,' her father continued. 'It's time she grew up.'

Anna's mum said nothing, had said nothing all this time, and for a moment, the only sound was the crashing of the dishes in the sink.

Unappeased, Anna's dad turned his attention to her. He pushed his face up close to hers. It was huge, red and shiny.

'Start eating like a human being!'

He crushed the hand she had been eating with in his, twisting the fork into a new position.

'Do you want us to send you to a psychiatrist? Well, do you?'

'Noooo,' Anna had wailed, tears falling down her face. She couldn't stop them. Oh, why couldn't she stop them?

'Bloody waterworks. I'll give you something to cry about,' he'd yelled, yanking her up from the chair.

The last thing Anna remembered from that night was the sound of her dad undoing his belt buckle.

THE WRITING PROJECT

Writing the child

Chapter 4 poetry

Experiment 4 (July-August 2017)
Reflections

My earliest tastes of poetry were in the form of children's rhymes in the old, battered board books I found in our toy box. Long after having outgrown those books, I would return to them, enjoying the feel of the rhymes and rhythms on my tongue, imagining myself reading them aloud in dulcet tones to an enthralled audience.

Poetry came to integrate itself into the rhythms of my life. Henry Kendall's 'Bellbirds'[1] attuned my ear to the tinkling calls of these birds. On every drive up the range to Toowoomba, I wind down the car window to listen for them. Snatches of verses from Susan Cooper's *The Dark is Rising* series come upon me at certain moments, such as on my last dig, where I found the line, 'wood, bronze, iron, water, fire, stone' in mind as my teammates and I trowelled small finds into the light of day.

Poetry pivots on the notion of the unique, providing 'specific insights into individualised personal human experience and linguistic expression'.[2] The desire to express myself and to gain insights into my own 'personal human experience' suggest that poetry is a form worth exploring for this writing experiment.

To begin, I look to exemplars with approaches that are tough, raw, no punches pulled, like Dorothy Porter's verse-novel *The Monkey's Mask*.[3] I want my poem to have impact, to slap the reader in the face, in the same way that a victim of domestic violence can be struck. Perhaps I will do this without warning, just as an abuser can strike without warning.

While I have no concept of what my poem will look like, I do sense what it will sound like. Punchy, punctuated, staccato: it will not be a thing of beauty but a glimpse into a violent moment in time. I will not treat the topic of domestic abuse politely, nicely, wrapping it up in soft cushioning. I want my poem to hit as hard as I have been hit.

My approach for this section follows those suggested in writing manuals, such as *Playing with Words*.[4] Read and analyse, imitate and develop. Then write your own. So, I will read more of Dorothy Porter's works and attempt this. I have written poetry, but that was all so long ago. Before I lost my creative self.

Now, however, because of these writing ventures, I am reconnecting with my past skills. I have reanimated my creative self. I am even growing closer to being able to read a full work of fiction, the first time in years.

I decide on a hidden narrative, where there is both a surface and underlying story. In this way, the real topic of domestic abuse will be unspoken yet embedded, hidden within another scene equally fraught with fear and thoughts of survival. This poem needs to be hard-hitting, direct, blunt, savage and shocking. I imagine incorporating sounds, or echo, to suggest the victim's perception of the smallness of the space in which the violence occurs: an insular, solitary bubble.

I am picturing a ship in a storm. Perhaps it is being torn apart; perhaps it only seems that way. Perhaps the reality is not made known. It may be a ship being wrecked on a reef, the result of poor judgement on behalf of the captain, or out of desperation to escape another danger.

I am fascinated by sailing ships of the past, especially those involved in long-distance travel. Ships that discovered new lands, such as Viking longboats and Iceland, Greenland and the northern parts of the Americas. I recently revisited the Rjiks Museum in Amsterdam. As with many of the galleries and museums I have visited, there are enormous paintings of sea battles, the artists capturing the violence of the scenes so effectively that I can almost smell the smoke, feel the booms of cannon fire, hear the vessels breaking apart.

Preparation

I begin with an idea-generating activity, brainstorming, to produce a repertoire of expressions to draw on in my upcoming poetry attempt.

Firstly, I will share with you the steps involved in brainstorming as I have taught it to both educators and students. It may be different from what you know or practice. I first met the concept when attending a post-graduate course on accelerated learning principles run by visiting academics from Germany. I wish I had known about it while at school and during my undergraduate studies. Today, brainstorming is a well-known tool. Over the years, I have developed my own approach.

To brainstorm is to generate as many ideas as possible on a chosen topic within a selected time frame. The rules for my version of brainstorming are:

- Set aside concerns about:

- selectivity - write down every idea/word that comes to mind (the selection process comes later)
- spelling (this can be rectified later)
- neatness (this is about maximum output, not tidiness)

- If you do not know the word in English, use the language you do know it in
- If you can picture it but do not know the word, draw it
- Focus only on the topic. If you have time to think of other matters during the brainstorming session, you have allocated too much time to it.

Brainstorming requires only a blank page/screen and a writing implement. There are Apps, too, for brainstorming. Having explored several of these for teaching and learning purposes, I can say these are not initially quick solutions. The time required to set up, learn the process, and the limitations as prescribed by the tools themselves are distractions from the goal of the brainstorming session. Using paper is fast. It is easy to write, draw, circle and connect; steps that come after the initial brainstorming session.

Choose a limited time for this process: brainstorming is about high energy and high output. The critical thinking comes afterwards. And remember, you can always do another brainstorming session as needed.

This is the process I follow. I have my materials at hand: paper, pencil, timer. I write the topic in the middle of the page, in this case, 'shipwreck', and set the timer. For the given time, I write down all the thoughts that come to mind. The result is a messy page hopefully full of ideas. This is followed by sorting, consideration, elimination, and selection. The main advantage of brainstorming is that ideas seemingly unrelated to the topic may in themselves become important. Or, the consideration of them may lead to other ideas. From there, key ideas and supporting elements are selected, and perhaps, a further brainstorming session is conducted on one of these identified elements. Content gathering may be necessary, such as general or detailed reading, watching of documentaries, or listening to interviews. It depends on the topic.

The aim of my brainstorming session is to generate not ideas on the topic, but a multitude of words and phrases, synonyms, antonyms, phrasal verbs, colloquialisms and standard language. These will form a word bank to draw on during the writing process, removing the need to search for expressions whilst writing.

......

I set myself five minutes. I was still in the depths of the process when the alarm sounded. This is encouraging, demonstrating an ability to be thoroughly involved in the process, and to be responsive to the topic. This is the result (the image below replicates the original, updated for clarity. You can find a photo of the original on my website):

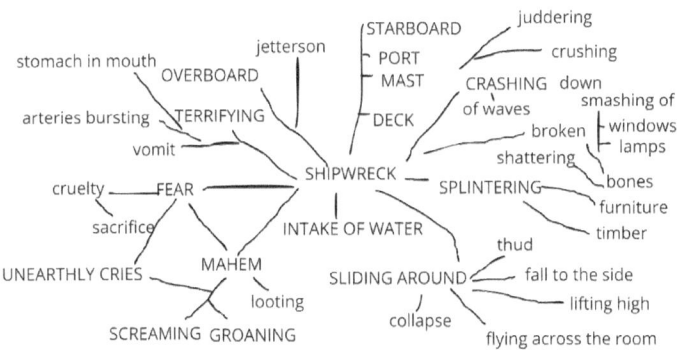

THE WRITING PROJECT

I note a lack of technical terms. Although I do have a few terms related to ships, there is space to add more. My next step is to arrange the words / phrases into categories to see what I need more of and where I have enough. I used a table for this (below). You can also categorise and arrange on the brainstorm page itself, using coloured pencils/pens to categorise by colour, or by circling, highlighting and the like. This is the result:

nouns/ noun phrases	bones timber furniture sliding around	unearthly cries thud	fear vomit stomach in mouth arteries bursting	cruelty
verbs	splintering shattering looting collapse	crushing screaming groaning	juddering ~~jetterson~~ jettison	
adjectives	~~mahem~~ mayhem broken	sacrifice terrifying		
verbal phrase	crashing down crashing of (waves)	fall to the side	lifting high flying across the room	intake (of water) smashing of windows, lamps
ship specific	starboard port deck mast	overboard		

You can see from my list that I was not concerned about keeping uniformity in my grammatical constructions. There is a mix of verb forms, for example, and this is because those were the words that came to mind. When I thought of 'splintering', for example, I thought not of a word to describe wood breaking; instead, I was hearing the wood blasting apart by force, hence the 'ing' form showing action. There is also a word unrelated to the others: cruelty. I cannot say why this word popped up, but it did. I have kept it on my list; it may allow me to pursue avenues such as personification, as in: 'will the cruelty of the storm's rage never cease?' or 'the act seemed so deliberate, so reeking of intentional cruelty, that surely there was a conscious mind driving it'. As well as an opportunity to eliminate and correct (as in the spelling of jettison), placing these words into a table allows me to see areas that need development.

It is clear I have few words related directly to ships, and only a few nouns. I would also like to add more phrasal verbs, those longer expressions that are very much a part of the vernacular, but which are often eliminated from academic writing. 'Tear apart' instead of fragment or shatter, for example. Using this word bank when writing my poem will allow me to concentrate my efforts on flow, rhythm, and possibly a rhyming scheme.

······

On the night of this brainstorming session I lay in bed, dreading the terrors that inhabit my sleep. I shifted my attention to what I could hear: the sounds of flying foxes, the breathing of my dogs. And then, lines of a poem came to mind.

I threw back the warm covers that lose their comfort when I

dream, feeling the cool air without. From the bookshelves lining one of my bedroom walls, I drew forth a writing pad and a pencil.

I wrote.

This may not become the finished poem I am after, but ...

I AM WRITING.

Desire to write! The drive to write!

The experiments are working.

The result is a piece with no particular form, but which captures the essence of the violence contained in one room, on what may or may not be a ship being tossed about in a storm.

> Palms clasped together, knees bending,
> I sink towards the floor in prayer.
>
> Eyes shut, not seeing the wall
> as my head crashes into hardwood panelling with shellac finish.
>
> The room is lurching, furniture splintering
> But the sound of screaming is dulled
> by the roaring of thunder in my ears.
>
> Hands grasping wildly, they gain no purchase
> My feet are not planted but floating in the air
> A lamp sails across the room and shatters into a thousand perilous pieces
> The lamp that belonged to my Great Aunt.
>
> Boom! The air is knocked from my lungs
> I am sinking, sinking
> Eyes open, I see a dark circle and many dots of light
> Are they stars? Am I looking at the open sky?
> Has the danger now passed?

With this piece now set out on a screen, I see I have employed imagery related to ships, the ocean, storms. My initial preparation helped greatly in allowing my mind to easily access these expressions without having to slow down the writing process to cast out for them.

My research supervisor asked a poet to read this piece. This was the poet's feedback.

> It is very explicit. You need some silences in this poem as there is nothing left for the reader's imagination. Avoid the verb to be. Images are good and striking – dots of light - aunt's lamp crashing to the floor… Avoid the obvious description… and let the imagery do its work.

While the aim of the experiments is to spark the **doing** of writing, not to produce crafted pieces, this is an opportunity to indulge in the reviewing/redrafting aspect of the writing process. This is something I enjoy. Before attempting to rework this piece, I sought further input from a group of peers, other researchers who meet to share and support one another. The members are from a variety of disciplines, ensuring the feedback is diverse.

One reaction was that the reader felt 'winded', meaning, I had partly achieved my aim: to convey the force of the attack for the victim. I took my peers' comments and used them to revise the piece, removing unnecessary words, such as 'together' (to clasp hands is to hold them together), and incorporating the advice of the poet to remove 'to be' in all its conjugations, although I do not entirely succeed in this.

The result is a piece of the same length, that conveys the same scene.

Palms clasped, knees bending,
I sink towards the floor.

Eyes shut in prayer
My head drums hollowly against the hardwood panelling
The sound of screaming is dulled
by the thundering in my ears.

The room lurches
My hands pluck at air but gain no purchase
My feet are floating, floating
A lamp sails across the room shattering into a thousand perilous pieces
The lamp of my late Great Aunt.

Boom! The air shudders
The breath is knocked from my lungs
I am sinking, sinking
Can you see that dark circle and those dots of light?
Are they stars? Is it the open sky?
Has the danger passed?

Discussion

Without expectation, the preparation for my poem awoke inspiration to write. Buoyed by this progress, I turn to Dorothy Porter's, *What a Piece of Work*.[5] In this verse novel, I sight the basis for another perspective on the theme of domestic abuse: the day after the storm.

I chose the chapter, 'Answered prayers' as my guide because of its simplicity. It suggests that the 'peace' referred to in the first line is the exception, not the norm. I intend to follow the piece's style, rhythm, and tone. I hope that in emulating a successful poet, that my creativity will continue to expand. Applying this method is extending my comfort zone, guiding me to write how I may not otherwise write.

I begin by creating a table with two columns, placing 'Answered prayers' in the column on the left. I will add my version in the column to the right. To initiate the writing process, I select the first line from 'Answered prayers', effecting a minor change. Almost immediately, I feel driven to use my own words, to say what I really feel, to let the truth come alive. Consequently, I add a third column. I write both my adaptation of the original, and my deviated, heartfelt version next to this, creating them simultaneously.

This is a liberating way to go beyond the task, yet fulfil the task. The outcome is two pieces, one which mirrors the original in many ways, and the other which has used the original's form as a springboard to a more variant piece. The first column with the exemplar is not displayed below, as I was unable to obtain permission from the publisher to reprint 'Answered prayers', in its entirety.

Sunday After

Version 1	**Version 2**
I do not 'believe the peace of this morning'[6]	I am not deceived by your calm demeanour
I ignore the wreckage It's not real	You walk over the wreckage And into the yard
I prepare us a breakfast tray And take it into the yard	I prepare a pot of tea The way you like it (or else)
The sky is perfection The sun is warm, so warm	The sky is vivid blue The sun growing in intensity
He loves the sun, I love the country air	You don't burn With your luscious olive skin
The sound of birds	It is the scorn beaming from your eyes that scorches my skin
He cradles the old china cup With a hand that hums with power	Your lips tighten and you screw up your nose The tea is not right, not right!
His gaze is distant Silently thinking those intelligent thoughts which are far beyond the rest of us	You hold my eyes I am entranced Even while the tea burns my face and stains my new white dress
This morning he is the perfectly rational human being He always claims to be	This morning you are the same person you always are Unpredictable, dissatisfied
This morning I am well-behaved	This morning, I am the same person I always am Useless, stupid
The obedient Subservient wife.	A spoilt little brat A peasant.[7]

I found this process exhilarating. Working from Porter's piece, whilst responding to my desire to write an alternate version, enabled me to grow beyond my limitations. I feel stronger.

Here, look, I have a new writing muscle.

I feel drawn to write more. When I began this project, every move was forced; once completed, I would fall flat from lack of impetus. Impetus is now within me, flowing through my veins: evidence of the efficacy of these writing experiments.

Reflections

Revisiting this chapter, I am reminded of the physical sensations of fear and panic I experienced when writing these poems. This was not writing from the intellect, but from the body. Celeste Snowber reminds us that we don't just 'have bodies; we are bodies': it is the body that cries, laughs, screams or bleeds.[1] Through writing, we transform embodied experiences into words.

This writing was more than imagination: I drew upon past experiences, imploding many incidents into a single event. Through this writing experiment, my creative expression reawakened. In doing writing, my lived experience and my creative expression combined to embrace my writing self. I played out the scenes in my mind, feeling them in my physical responses, transmuting them into written words. This represented true depth of engagement in the creative writing process, true enactment of writing not only for the self, but of the self.

POETRY

Writing muscles

Chapter 5 fairy tale

Experiment 5 (September-November 2017)
Extemporaneous writing
Reflections

In the past, I took refuge in imaginary worlds through reading and writing, the mystique of myths and legends often informing my thoughts. When I was twelve years old, in my second year of high school, my English teacher brought a trolley of books to class to encourage extracurricular reading. Eagerly, I selected a YA version of *The Odyssey*. My teacher, however, was visibly disappointed. She encouraged me to reconsider, offering me an alternate book. However, I took no notice, so keen was I to indulge in Greek mythology.

In that moment, I chose to follow my personal interests rather than reading a book that may have developed my intellect or reading ability. Instead, *The Odyssey* set me off on further forays into imaginary worlds which became both sanctuary and trap. These worlds provided an escape from my home life, the violence, the uncertainty, the lies, the sexual tension, the manipulation, all of which confounded me. I had no capacity to sort through it or see beyond it. I had no choice but to accept the blame placed upon my young shoulders for family and household issues, from my older sister losing her door key when she was out walking, to the breakdown of the 20-year-old oven. I lived in fear of random punishments. There was no guidance, no positive role model, no explanations to help me through. Perhaps I could have found such a role model in the right readings. Perhaps that is what my teacher was trying to achieve. As it was, mythology - and its extension, fantasy - was my escape.

In preparing to write my fairy tale, I turn to modern writers for inspiration, and perhaps to act as models. A.S. Byatt's writing reflects a deep knowledge of symbolism, an important aspect of the fairy tale. Her short story, 'The thing in the forest',[1] incorporates these and other elements of the fairy tale, such as the monster, to highlight the human condition. I particularly admire her intense attention to detail when describing nature, although what she chooses the children to see often shocks me.

For example, in the forest, the girls see berries that are 'dead-flesh purple … and some like pieces of meat protruding from tree-trunks'. It is as if the little girls' world reflects the greater horrors of the war that was killing, maiming, destroying families, hopes and innocence. And the 'worm' is as far removed from the romantic portrayal of a dragon as possible. Instead, it is the conglomeration of all that a child would find revolting.

What disturbs me even more is the use of one phrase when describing the stench that precedes the worm, 'unwashed trousers', which is noted earlier in the story when describing the seats on the train. The story is set in an era when very few women wore trousers, and so the unwashed trouser smell is the smell of men's unwashed trousers. Why would little girls be comparing the smells about them to that of men's unwashed trousers? Byatt is intending to shock, to make the reader ask herself questions. This is truly talented writing. And far beyond not only my ability, but also my aim, which is to tell a simpler story, one that is based on my lived experience.²

Next, I turn to Angela Carter's stories. These are also the outcome of intelligence and talent. Carter weaves fabulous narrative out of imagination, knowledge of language and storytelling. She combines elements from fairy tales, mythology, and everyday life to create horror stories. 'The bloody chamber',³ turns the story of 'Bluebeard' into a horror story with a 'happy' ending of marriage. But that is not the point I take from the story. It is the fact that the about-to-be-murdered child-bride is saved by her gun toting, horse riding mother. It is this element that seeps into my psyche like minerals into an underground waterway. A female hero is a new take, but all the same, the rescue arrives, as in many fairy tales, from outside. And my story has no such hero.

······

My attempt at writing unleashes memories accompanied by distress. I can write no more. Instead, I hide away in procrastination, frittering away my precious time. It is here that I turn to an examination of self-regulation as a way forward. Writing, like all voluntary activities, requires self-regulation: it is 'self-planned, self-initiated, and self-sustained'.⁴ The emphasis is on 'self'. If I want to develop new writing habits, I need to develop high levels of self-regulation. This is particularly important where the writing topic is emotionally triggering.

After speaking with my supervisor to set up a strict deadline, creating a strong sense of accountability, and reducing distractions in my writing environment, I am ready to re-attempt writing my fairy tale. Here is the result:

Fairy tale

Once upon a time there was a princess who lived in a shiny new castle in the hills. There were many such castles about the place. Her father, like the owners of all the other castles, was a minor king. A king only when in his own castle, you could say. But king all the same.

The king had children: three princesses. Three lovely girls. But no son. The king was fretful about not having a son, for he so wanted to bring him up just as his father had raised him.

You're the son, he told the middle princess. I will mould you in my own shape. I don't care about the others, they can marry. But you will do all that I couldn't, you will become all that I wished to be. It will be you who sets forth to conquer other kingdoms, who brings fame to our family.

The middle princess heard what her father had to say. She looked at him with the large eyes that all children have and felt proud to be the chosen one. Her sisters were filled with envy because they both wanted to be the apple of their father's eye.

A few years later, the little princess was playing with her toys. Her father, the king, had been watching her for some time, but she hadn't known it.

He walked over to her and picked her up by the collar.

The princess felt scared. The king looked angry, but she didn't know why. She was a sweet child, with childish thoughts. But this is not what the king wanted. He stared hard at her chest.

Finally, he set her down on her feet and spoke.

You are too old to be playing with toys.

He was angry. So angry. And the princess, being scared,

began to cry.

Suddenly the princess was moving backwards across the room, her feet off the ground.

The king was holding her up against the wall.

Do you want me to give you something to cry about? he said, his face pressed up to hers. His face was red, swollen, his eyes puffy and his fleshy cheeks were wobbling. His spit stuck to her face.

Nooooo, the princess responded in a tiny, tiny voice. The tiny voice of a child.

Frank, he boomed.

The princess could hear footsteps approaching the room. Angry footsteps.

Yes, George, came her mother's voice. She hated being called Frank. Her name was Frances.

The king let go of the princess so her feet could touch the floor. He turned around and yelled at her mother.

Teach your daughter how to act like an adult.

As he stormed from the room, he added, Get her a bra.

...

The next day the princess was taken for a drive by her mother.

Where are we going, mum? she asked.

Nowhere, her mother growled.

Her mother looked angry. She was muttering to herself.

Her mother was a nervous driver, always worrying about the cars behind her. She felt they were out to get her, tailgating her, trying to force her moves.

The princess didn't like driving with her mother. Or with the king, for that matter, as he paid little attention to the road and instead, drove along pointing out all the features of the area. Whenever the princess spoke out to warn her father of a danger, he would bellow at her, become red in the face, and sometimes raise his left hand to her own small face. The backhand, he called it. Like in tennis.

But this day, the destination was a mystery, and so the princess focussed on the positive aspects of that situation. Going somewhere new? Doing something different? She pondered and imagined and then they had arrived. It was the local department store.

Shopping! she cried in delight.

Her mother's mutters became louder. The princess could only make out some words, and those that she could filled her with dread. Kill him, bastard, mutter, mutter.

The princess, fighting back tears, put on the show of a happy face. She was a princess after all. And if her father heard back that someone had seen her looking anything other than perfectly happy … well, she had experienced that, and had learnt her lesson.

It had been her parents' friends, the wife, to be exact, that had carried the tale to her father. Why she had felt it her need to do so was beyond the princess's comprehension. All she knew was that she must always were a mask of happiness, especially around the women in her life. They would betray her, as her sisters and mother did, or criticise her and scold her for feeling what she felt. There was no-one she could reveal her true feelings to. She didn't lock those feelings away, she simply failed to acknowledge them anymore. The princess was learning well: she was able to experience physical pain yet smile; she could be insulted yet act as if she hadn't heard it. She had yet to master her excitement about shopping.

As she and her mother passed through the department store, the princess's eyes swivelled about her, desperately trying to see what attracted so many shoppers.

The princess, led by her mother, stopped in an area that the princess had never seen before. There were racks and racks of flimsy garments that held no interest for her. While her mother was speaking with an attendant, the princess slipped over to the escalators and looked down to the floors below, longing to visit the toys, the games, the …

Get over here now, came her mother's voice. Not an invitation, but a warning.

Can I tell you what went on next? Expose you to the tedium of being fitted for a bra, of the humiliation of being spoken about like a piece of meat by the attendant and your mother, of the angry growls and embarrassing mutterings of your mother when it came to pay for the purchase.

You'd better make it last, growled the princess's mother as they moved at speed through the store to the car park.

Yes, mum, said the princess, again holding back tears.

That night the princess was sent for by the king. She stood and listened to the ranting and raving. She had embarrassed her mother in public. She had refused to be grateful. She was lucky wasn't a boy because, if she was, she'd get a bashing, just like his father gave him. As it was, she would be treated to a mere beating. A treat indeed.

After the beating, the princess quietly walked from the room. As she did so, she noticed that her mother had been there all the time. She was standing at the window in the far corner of the room, busily scrubbing at a spot on the frame.

The princess walked over to her mother - a hug would make all the difference.

Mum, she said softly.

The mother of the princess didn't stop scrubbing. The princess could see that her mother's face was dark with anger. Against her? She responded without looking at the princess, emitting a deep, ugly growl that formed the words, don't involve me.

The princess couldn't maintain her composure any longer. She ran from the room. While she passed along the same corridor on the way to her room as always, it seemed a different place. Almost as if she was heading downwards, down there, towards the dungeon.

I don't understand, I don't understand, she kept repeating to herself. I don't understand.

One day, the princess was sitting at her little table looking at her books. Oh, how she longed to play with her toys.

Her mother entered her room. She was smiling.

Come along, girl, she said in a happy tone that the princess had rarely heard her use. We have a guest.

The princess stood up and her mother stopped her. Turn around, she said.

As the princess turned on the spot, her mother looked her over.

Yes, that will do.

Together they walked to the great hall where the king was talking to someone.

This is my daughter, the king said, grandly gesturing to the princess.

This is prince ..., said her father. He is to be your husband.

The princess, unable to control her horror, replied, But he's a frog!

The king's face immediately grew red and blotchy. The princess' mother slipped into the background, and the princess was left standing all alone.

Come, come now, young lady, said the frog. I am going to take care of you from now on. Your father has been telling me how precious you are, like a son to him, in fact.

The frog approached the princess and stood directly in front of her. He was a foot shorter than her, and his eyes were level with the little shelf in her dress made by that contraption of a bra she was forced to wear.

You should obey your parents, moaned the frog, and the princess realised, with revulsion, that her shoes were filling with his saliva. His eyes were focussed on her little shelf and from his open mouth the drool poured in thick, green rivulets.

The princess, terrified, smiled all the same. This is what she had been trained to do.

Her father was watching her intensely. His body, taught like a spring, was slightly raised in his chair. The princess knew what the look in his eyes meant. If she were to embarrass him, he would have her beaten. Or locked in the dungeon. She took a deep breath. The princess smiled differently, moving her chin to one side, flashing a flirtatious glance at the frog.

Well, my dear, when is the happy day to be?

Tonight, came her father's voice, followed by a guttural laugh.

Tonight, echoed the frog, drool pooling around his feet.

Organise it, yelled the king to his wife, who stormed from the room, her mutterings following her along the corridor.

Until tonight, said the princess and bowed slightly before turning elegantly on her heel and leaving the room.

Once back in her chamber, the princess dropped her hidden panic on the smooth, marble floor.

She paced back and forth, wailing, for what was she to do? With not one person of trust to turn to.

She knew this was her own fault. Her father had been so affected by her failure to gain the top award in her studies that he gave up all thoughts of her as his son and heir. She knew she had failed him. But with no one to guide her, no mentors, no advice, she had floundered along, doing what she thought was right, but which was never right.

And now he was passing her off onto that. Frog.

The princess finally stopped and looked in the mirror. Reflected in the glass was another face, one that looked like her mum but that wasn't her mum. It was her own face, 30 years on.

He's not fit to lick your shoe, the older self said to the princess. None of them are. They are bad, bad people. Save yourself, for no matter what you do to please them, they will only continue to hurt you. The frog will rape you every day for the rest of your life. If you stay.

But I know no other way, cried the princess, scared, so scared, of not doing what was expected of her.

If you leave this place, assured the older self, you will find your people. Not immediately, not successfully at first, not for a very long time, but one day you will. Leave and establish your own kingdom. Be kind to others that are powerless like you have been.

The princess was frozen with fear. She could not believe.

She could not.

Her older self spoke. I will be there tonight. Accept my gift before those of anyone else, and you will know what to do.

That night, the princess was taken from her chamber by her two giggling sisters who spoke of cock and semen, and the pain of losing her virginity. The princess said nothing. Holding her gaze down, she allowed herself to be swept along, until she was in the great hall.

The room was filled with the ugliness of leering men and fat, envious wives. She heard their lewd comments and their filthy criticisms: too thin, too small chested, too this, too that. She looked about but could not see the older self she had seen in her mirror. Her heart sank.

She was taking her position next to the frog when the doors and windows of the room flew open and the bowl of punch shattered, sending pink sticky liquid across the dresses of the fat, envious women.

As the room dissolved into chaos, the princess felt a gentle touch on her arm.

Here, said her older self. My gift to you.

The princess took the long package and tore off the wrappings.

Inside was a fairway woods club. Her father had never allowed her to play golf, telling her it was not a sport for girls, but she had always fancied herself a golfer and had once secretly attended a private lesson.

The princess was admiring the club when she realised that, amidst the chaos, the frog was watching her. He marched towards her, one hand deep in the pocket of his trousers, drawing attention to the tent like protuberance in front. The princess turned slightly to her side, stepped forward, and swung the club. The frog smashed into a glutinous mush that plastered faces, hair and clothes.

She turned on her heal and left, flicking squished frog off her face, standing taller than she ever had before. She left the castle with nothing more than her golf club and never returned.

Discussion

Exploring this genre, and particularly, the act of writing, uncovered hidden beliefs which had impacted the way I lived my life. These revelations prompted both physical and emotional discomfort.

I responded to this intense discomfort initially by avoiding the writing process through procrastination. While procrastination is often referred to **as** writing block,[5] this is incorrect. Procrastination is a recourse, a default position, when writers or would-be writers have some reason for not engaging in the writing process. Such reasons include fear of failure, poor planning, a lack of understanding of the task, or even resentment of the task, and these can mostly fall under the broad label of lack of self-regulation. Procrastination allows us to temporarily avoid addressing our reasons for not writing, to justify our non-commitment to the task. In my case, it was the intense discomfort and a sense of overwhelm following memories and associated emotions of my lived experience of domestic abuse. I found my way forward by applying the principles of self-regulation. Had I been experiencing true writing block, like the complete block that inspired this research project, then no amount of self-regulation would have succeeded to move me into the fundamental element of the creative writing process: the desire to write. In this case, I had the desire, but held back because of painful emotions.

Avoidance through procrastination, not block.

I approached this experiment intending to explore a genre as a way of sparking entry into the creative writing process, perhaps even seeing this practice materialise in my everyday life. This occurred in an unexpected way: as writing that I felt in my body. It came with force, this transition into embodied writing. Because of this unexpected outcome, and because I am now able to use creative writing as a tool to express myself and as a strategy to take charge of my story, I am ready to address the issues of trauma writing and writing trauma.

Extemporaneous writing (November 2017)

I see things of beauty all around, and I do, because I was born with an eye for happiness. I absorb those things of beauty into my soul where they fall flat and die. In that space there is no air, no light. Nothing can survive.

In my soul there are piles of skeletons, the remains of loved ones I was unable to say goodbye to in the only way I knew how.

In my soul there are pools of toxic waste, colours and perfumes that have corroded, lying unused, useless, feeling unwanted, unappreciated, unvalued.

In my soul there is a stench, the vile compilation of years of neglect, unexpressed desire, pain, joy, unresolved confusion.

I carry this inside me, and as the years pass, the burden of its increasing weight pulls me down. Poison is leaching into my body, inviting disease.

The diseases increase with the years, and I'm afraid that my life has passed me by. Soon I will be no more than a shell, a once-was person. I move along, forward, moving, keep moving. I fought for justice, but the toll was greater than I imagined it could be. Can a shadow live a life complete?

Reflections

On returning to this chapter after all these years, I am awed, once again, at the transformative qualities of writing. Had I not sat with this genre, had I continued to evade the discomfort it awoke in me, I would have missed an opportunity to gain deep personal insight. The pretence by females in the society I grew up in is not only in response to men: it is women who perpetuate it and benefit from it, keeping themselves, and others, repressed. I see not only the confusion and fear of the princess in this story, but also the lost opportunities of the sisters who embrace their limited, petty roles. And there is the long-suffering mother, whose misery has become so much of her being, welling forth in barely audible mutterings that reveal profanities and murderous intentions.

Clarissa Pinkola Estes says, 'when a woman pretends to press her life down into a nice tidy little package, all she accomplishes is spring-loading all her vital energy down into shadow'.[1] The mother in this story has crammed her 'vital energy down' for so long that it is surfacing without her realising it, toxic fumes erupting as angry mutterings. There can be no room for kindness and compassion until she allows her own spirit to rise into the light.

The power of writing as facilitator of truth and myth, exploration of the inner and the outer, drew into the light a personal understanding that is also a social one. I grew to understand what Marilyn French, in *The War Against Women*, meant when she said that 'individual violence [against women] could not be as widespread and devastating without broad-scale support'.[2] Domestic abuse could not continue if the 'broad-scale support' we lend it as pretenders, as unobjecting observers, as role-players, as non-defenders of daughters, sisters, mothers came to an end. Until we realise the roles we play, until we find the strength to question our support (overt or covert) of the systems that oppress, until we are willing to incur the disdain of those who would sustain oppression, positive, lasting change will not occur.

Have I told you that I based the mother in the fairy tale on my own mother? For years, I saved with one goal in mind: to liberate my mother from her life of suffering. However, once I had secured a loan and an apartment for her, she flatly turned me down. She told me she had 'grown used to it'. Offered an option (my option, not one of her own making), she chose to stay. I picture her as I last saw her, hunched over upon herself, her body protecting her heart. She did whatever it took to protect herself, erasing uncomfortable truths to make room for more digestible untruths. And yet, while I wanted to save my mother, I did not see the reality of my own life: that I too had lived with monstrous abuse; that I, too had acted as though there was nothing wrong.

Estes says that 'trying to be good, orderly, and compliant in the face of inner or outer peril ... de-souls a woman. It cuts her from knowing; it cuts her from her ability to act ... normalising the abnormal.'[3]

The act of writing about this aspect of domestic abuse, the mask-wearing, the pretence, the expectations placed on the female child, the stifling of her inner self, sparked a connection with 'knowing'. Through that act of writing, I was able to gain perspective on these aspects of domestic abuse, and to start the search for an authentic self where I no longer lived a life 'normalising the abnormal'.

THE WRITING PROJECT

Writing as listening to my soul

Chapter 6 essential pause

On Writing Trauma and Trauma Writing (December 2017-January 2018) Reflections

So far, each chapter has represented a new writing experiment. This one does not. Instead, I take an essential pause to discuss this writing place I now inhabit.

I am bruised and sore, yet my mind is willing to embark on flights of fancy, feeling freer to set out on adventure. Exploring the fairy tale took me into unknown territory which elicited a myriad of unexpected responses. Memories arose as a series of cesspools transforming the landscape into a wasteland. These memories evoked a range of emotional and physical sensations – a consort of disparate feelings that functioned independently and without awareness of each other. It was if Snow White entered the forest for a gentle stroll, only to be attacked by animals, birds, insects, rocks, trees, plants, and the weather, each determined to do their part regardless of what else was occurring. How does one fend for oneself in such a confusion?

The fight or flight response is spoken about ad nauseum. However, natural responses also include immobilisation,[1] or freezing. Freezing has always been my reflexive response. From infancy, I was conditioned to not protect myself, to become limp when being threatened or beaten. I have tried to break this response, tried many times to retrain my mind to protect my body. Oh, how I have wished for my body to respond with fight, with fire. In my late teens, after leaving home, I attended multiple self-defence courses; the beatings from my boyfriend continued. Self-defence training is directed at fending off an unknown predator: a stranger (in the street, pub, bus stop). It involves knowing how to respond to a variety of scenarios: an arm around the neck, a hand on the wrist.

But what about when an electrical fault has switched off your lights (or so you think) when you are in the shower? Do you expect an attacker to be outside the bathroom door? Are you armed with your variety of responses for the street, pub, bus stop when wrapped in a towel opening your bathroom door in your own home? Thinking there is nothing much the matter, only the electricity has switched off, which it does on occasion? A planned attack by a person familiar with your house, your dogs, your habits, your behaviours. A person who knows his way into the house without a key. A person driven by greed, lust, an overwhelming need to control.

Where is the training for that?

Submitting, fainting, or feigning fainting is an unconscious response, which occurs when options such as fighting or running away are not possible.[2] While the outcome may mean survival, this instinctive response has been linked to the onset of post-traumatic stress disorder (PTSD),[3] and other physical disorders such as bowel issues.[4] Freezing as a response may have saved my life. It was, however, seized upon by the legal defence for the rapist, used as evidence against me in court. My 'failure' to attempt to fight off my attacker, to bite him, to cry out 'Murder! Murder!' was converted into a case for my complicity.

Writing the fairy tale was to wander through the rooms of a medieval manor house, opening doors, stepping into and out of light, finding rooms that sucked the breath out of me, and others that made me gasp. Some doors had been closed deliberately, sealed, never to be reopened. The fairy tale as a genre was the key to unlocking them. I returned there, to those rooms, not with my thinking mind but with my body. I did not understand at the time of writing that I was 'writing trauma'. This is where in, through, during, and after the act of writing, trauma is reanimated within the body and the unconscious mind, even if the conscious mind does not understand what is happening.

One Australian writer says of her own experience that telling a story based on trauma 'engenders the stirring up … of the original traumatic events.'[5] She refers to her own body's responses and reactions as 'trauma body', 'those physical parts … that respond with encrypted messages before the rest of me even knows there's anything going on.'[6] I experienced this trauma body during the creative writing process of the fairy tale. Fortunately, owing to treatment with a trauma specialist, I was able to recognise my physical and emotional responses as connected to past events, ones that she could help me reappraise. Until I was able to obtain an appointment with her, however, I experienced weeks of bombardment on my body (shudders, pain), and unexpected, sudden outbursts of intense emotion. Momentary glimpses of peace came only when I was fully occupied in the moment, such as during a yoga pose. I found this period extremely difficult. Less so than in the past, however, when I did not understand what was happening to me, when I struggled along without reprieve. Knowledge and experience are essential to surviving the writing trauma process.

In *The Body Keeps the Score*,[7] Bessel van der Kolk examines how past trauma affects our bodies, manifesting in diseases that can, and do, kill people. Such diseases for women are often connected with autoimmunity, precipitating related health disorders and diminishing of physical ability. Following van der Kolk, the inability to protect oneself from ongoing danger results in the body believing that being attacked is the natural order. In line with this theory, I could say that my immune system lay siege to my thyroid, making manifest the constant attack against my need to speak out. This silencing was carried out by both those who were supposed to protect me, and those who had harmed me. In perpetuating this silencing, did my body's immune system become my enemy? I do not believe so: I believe this was just another form of self-protection, removing my ability to fight or flee, and instead, reinforcing silence and stillness.

In contrast to writing trauma, trauma writing is considered therapeutic. It is an approach used under professional guidance. While there is evidence that trauma writing has the potential to result in positive effects, there have been few studies examining trauma writing and PTSD.[8] Writing about our trauma can be cathartic, but it can also be the opposite.[9] Even the eliciting of emotion by a therapist can cause harm to a client unless it occurs with a reappraisal of that trauma.[10] Consequently, trauma writing is not an appropriate choice for all trauma victims.

Exploring the fairy tale as a genre lead me to writing trauma. This, in turn, permitted and encouraged the shedding of light onto pervasive wrongs, beliefs and happenings. Drawn out of their caves, named, and confronted, these wrongs have lost some of their hold over me. This has been a painful yet rewarding experience. My engagement in the process of writing a fairy tale and the responses that arose might be described as 'reflexivity', the 'bidirectional relationship between cause and effect, where both the cause and the effect form a dynamic that moves the inquiry forward'.[11] In my case, this is where the writer, the act of writing, and the written product are mutually supportive, working together in a type of synergy.[12]

The result? I feel prepared to return to my writing practice, to set out some of my experience, to finally engage in some **trauma writing**. I hope to isolate more of the putrid, abhorrent and toxic sludge from my mind and body. I will put it onto the page, see it and manipulate it, to reduce the effect it has over me. To do this is to use writing as a positive strategy to improve my life.

A final word, and a warning

One Australian researcher says of her personal experience of writing trauma, 'while it may be useful, such purging of the soul can leave behind a dark, pervasive rancour. When you drag up the past with gut-wrenching fierce anger and pain, it's bound to create a cloud of constant recollection.'[13] It could also result in something worse, where 'telling the ghastly tale may, in some cases, trigger not only serious somatic trouble, psychotic episodes, but suicide'.[14]

I have been fortunate in having access a therapist to help me cope with the physical and emotional responses arising from writing a fairy tale and reawakening a nightmare. I would not recommend undertaking writing trauma (or trauma writing) to anyone without professional guidance. I did not know that exploring the fairy tale would be the key to unlocking so much trauma. This is the magic, and perhaps the danger, of writing – it allows us to discover and to uncover.

Had I known what exploring this genre would reveal, perhaps I would have avoided it, and in doing so, missed an opportunity to grow. Now that it is done, however, I am much further along my journey to becoming the writer of the self that I once was.

Reflections

> *What child raises her arm in defence against an adult male? I imagine the courage of such an act, cringe at imagining the violent repercussions. Such bravery only antagonises the brute. Such a child does not reproduce brave children. Such a child does not live to grow up. I am the child that did live to grow up. That was not brave. I melted away whatever I needed to, to survive. I, too, will not reproduce, for I refuse to continue the cycle.*

For the past 20 years, I have been volunteering in the rehabilitation and care of rescued dogs. Initially, with cruelty cases at the RSPCA, then as a foster carer in my own home. I have seen so many different personalities, so much that suggests to me of past experiences. Some dogs react to triggers, actions they associate with abuse, such as the raising of a hand, the slamming of a door, a certain tone of voice. Some dogs never stop responding in fear to those triggers. Many, however, do. I help them to retrain. They change.

I wonder why it is that I have never been able to unlearn my own childhood conditioning, why I have never been able to step in and raise an arm in my own defence, despite professional guidance, training and encouragement. I do not have an answer for this, although Bessel van der Kolk says our bodies adjust to accept the repeated trauma we are unable to defend ourselves against.[1] As a result, our natural protective instincts switch off, and remain so, even when the source of the danger changes.

I write, in the following, of one of my (failed) attempts to retrain body and mind.

South Korea, 1997

I've been training privately, three times a week in two-hour blocks, with a Taekkyon master. For six hours a week I've been learning first moves, then combinations of moves to form patterns: solo dancing in one direction, then another. It is more like ChiGong than Taekwondo. I enjoy it, although I have no talent for learning patterns, and never remember them from one session to the next.

After three months, the instructor indicates he has taken me as far as he can. It is time to grade, and join the group classes. To prepare me for the upcoming grading, he hires a young female black belt to introduce me to sparring. It is time to put those graceful, dance-like moves into action. Each time the young woman steps towards me, very slowly, very gently raising an arm, or a leg, I freeze. We try again, and again, but I cannot raise an arm or a leg in self-defence. My limbs are logs, I cannot breathe, my stomach sinks.

However, the master does not give up on me, and with the next session comes a new addition to my training team: a small boy. He's perhaps eight, though he could easily be six, he's so small. Here I am, the master watching, the young black belt watching. The boy strikes my limp body, over and over. I stand there, motionless, receiving blow after blow, until the master instructs the boy to stop.

I leave that day and never return.

ESSENTIAL PAUSE

Writing and righting my life

Chapter 7 Trauma Writing

Experiment 6 (February 2018)
Reflections

Until now, I have started each experiment by selecting a genre and form, with this initiating or guiding my writing attempts, even while those attempts have strayed into other forms/styles. For this chapter, I commenced writing without a structure in mind. I simply wrote organically. Perhaps this at-will writing indicates the experiments are no longer needed. I feel it is too early to tell. What

I do know is I am writing more in my everyday life, about my frustrations, my joys, and my losses. Still, I fear this writing is but a mirage: it will disappear if I take my eyes off it. For that reason, I must continue with the writing experiments. I must be certain that my writing self is, once again, an integral part of who I am.

'Testimony', the piece I wrote for this chapter, is not included here. Written as trauma writing, it is a messy piece, more emotion than story. It is difficult to follow, lacks logic in its structure, and is terrible writing. This is because its purpose was therapeutic: it was not about the writing product, but the **doing** of the writing, transmuting emotions and physical responses into language. As trauma writing, there is to be no audience other than myself.

In lieu, I offer the image at the beginning of this chapter. This word cloud, produced using NVivo, qualitative data analysis software, provides a summary of the content via the most frequently used words in the text. The more frequent the word, the larger it is. The word count of the final draft was 1490 words.

Discussion

The initial writing of this piece poured out of me in response to an article I was reading. This article discussed using testimony as a form of writing about trauma. Testimony as a form is 'important because of what it does, its impact, rather than its truthfulness.'[1]

The story I wrote is not 'true' in that the witness providing the testimony, the narrator, is a fictional character, a composite of several people. Those people and their responses served to intensify the trauma experienced by the victim. This story provides testimony, bearing witness to a part of the trauma that enmeshed the victim: that which occurred in the many betrayals by friends, colleagues, associates and loved ones.

Writing this story was a means of moving some of the intensity out of my mind and body and onto the page. As written words, I could see the story, manipulate it, and take control of it. In this way, I gained distance. I noted the repetition of some elements previously mentioned in other pieces. Returning to them means they are still with me, still hold sway over me. Writing about them, however, encourages change. It does not cure the pain, does not diminish in any way my cruel treatment by some very revolting people. However, writing about my experiences, then reworking that writing, does allow me to engage with those experiences in different ways. The memories and embodied reactions are no longer a threat, a vulture in my head eternally circling, casting a shadow on my thoughts and memories.

Through writing, I am empowered to take charge of these feelings. I can be erudite or coarse, clever or monotonous. The use of language as written words allows me freedom and control. And control is something victims of abuse often have very little of. Through my writing experiments, I am regaining a sense of agency. I am taking in hand the impact of the trauma, writing to make sense of my world.

Notes from Research Journal (22 Feb 2018)

Yesterday ... some organic writing bubbled out of me and onto the page. I wrote and wrote until my exhaustion signalled it was time to stop.

The initial writing onto paper was difficult; the words were at times hard to read, I wrote so quickly.

But transcribing this today, I found myself rarely looking at the words. The story took on new forms, altering at the touch of my fingers without the deep venturing into emotion of yesterday's writing. This is power; this is control.

I am now the creator, not only the victim and observer. If I wish, I can paint the demons in excrement. It is my creation now, not only my story.

What a joy. What a relief.

Reflections

I reread 'Testimony', the piece you have not seen, and find it so different from the preceding pieces. It was undertaken as writing as therapy, or trauma writing, and I note that it filled this purpose effectively. Through the process of writing, I gave acknowledgement to 'the body as a wise source and experience of information'.[1] I listened to the gut instinct stifled by the 'normalisation of violence'[2] that comes from a life in which domestic abuse is as common as household duties.

Trauma writing enables the reconnection of body and mind. Through this new, open dialogue, I have learnt to listen to the pain of holding back the impulse to run, to scream, to shake in fear, to hold my hands up in defence. Consequently, the piece as a written product does not align with a specific genre or form, nor is it well-written. It is confusing to read. It is the process, not the product, that offers an effective trauma writing experience.

My readings about, and experience of, writing trauma and trauma writing have served to remind me of one of the most significant roles of my former writing practice. Writing was a means of making sense of my world, of processing experiences, of shapeshifting what could not be altered in real life. This type of writing holds medicinal qualities: it is able to heal, able to replenish. In its rawest form, it is personal and is never written for an audience other than the self. Consequently, I removed the piece I wrote organically after exploring the ideas of writing trauma and trauma writing: the written product was for me alone.

This is not to say that you cannot take what you have written and craft it into a piece for an external audience. Of course, you can. Sharing your story may help others.[3] And perhaps I will do this myself, one day. But this would be a separate action, removed from the original purpose of trauma writing, which is purely writing for the self. Despite the almost overwhelming notion of 'writer' as someone who writes for an audience, a person who writes to be published, the 'I' that is the trauma writer writes only for the one true audience of this approach: the self.

THE WRITING PROJECT

There is power in the doing of writing

Chapter 8 horror

Experiment 7 (February-March 2018)
Reflections

Since finalising my exploration of the fairy tale, I have been writing more and more in my everyday life. I am drawn to revisit one of the stories I read in preparation for the fairy tale: 'The bloody chamber' by Angela Carter. This story offers a useful format for exploring intimate partner abuse. A clever reworking of 'Bluebeard', the story provides an ending where the wife is saved by her mother. She then goes on to marry for love. In the story as first written for publication by Charles Perrault,[1] there are morals attached to the story – a woman's curiosity can get her killed, and a woman should obey her husband.

What I see when I read Perrault's version is a house filled with the wife's family who do nothing to help her, other than a sister signalling to their absent brothers. Honestly, a house full of people against one man? Why did they not act together and rescue the wife? The complacency exhibited by the wife's family and friends is not only found in fairy tales: I grew up with it.

I want to tell you a story. When I was 15, I was terrorised by a group of men. I never knew who they were. Nightly, they drove past our corner house, yelling obscenities combined with my name.

This lasted for weeks. I lived in fear of being abducted, gang raped, murdered. Shallow grave in nearby bushland. My father refused to call the police; I was not allowed to, threated by my father, his hand raised in my face. He said if we reported them, they would throw a brick through the window. Making himself yet another nighttime snack, he told me to address it myself, to 'tell those older men you know' to stop doing it. This, from the man who had been telling me since I could walk, 'Don't you get yourself raped'. My mother said and did nothing. To my eternal gratitude, my friend's older brother and his mates lay in wait for that car of men one night. After following the car, catching and confronting the men, the stalking stopped.

And so, the story of 'Bluebeard', with its exposure of a family abdicating responsibility for a daughter's safety, lies close to my heart. I attempt to rewrite it following Angela Carter's style. I enjoy the process, writing over 2,000 words in one sitting. However, I am unable to produce a suitable end to the story. It needs to be different from the original, and from Carter's, but how to highlight the theme of domestic abuse in my own, unique way?

I decide to leave the story for a few days, continuing instead with other elements of my research. As I do, my ideas find room to dissemble, reassemble, evolve, and change. Time away from writing is thus constructive. This has been referred to as *active silence* and *essential delay*.[2] Ursula Le Guin describes it beautifully as 'the wordless silence of germination'.[3]

Eventually, I decide to create and follow a plan:
- Marries
- Told not to go into his office
- Does not, has no interest
- On marriage, he persuades her to allow him to manage her finances

- He cuts off her access to funds, to the outside world
- He doesn't allow friends to visit. Once, a friend slips in as a delivery arrives, and he finds them together, two women chatting together happily at the tea table.
- He makes a scene
- After friend leaves, he demands sex, throwing down an open sex magazine, demanding 'that' position.
- He's a brute, constantly arriving home at odd hours demanding sex.
- The longer she is married to him, the more she is repulsed by him
- She finds she loses hours, even days on end. He convinces her she's insane.
- One day she borrows a phone belonging to a tradie and calls her bank. Sorry, madam, we have no accounts in your name. Can you check? No, those accounts have all been closed.
- She spends her time with her pet …?
- He is jealous, says You love it more than you love me …
- One day, she finds the pet has been poisoned …
- Desperate to call the RSPCA for help, she breaks into his office, climbing out of one window and carefully easing her way, outside the walls, into his office, to use the phone.
- Discovers the rumours were true – his finances were in a state of disarray. He had been borrowing money from one source, to pay another, and had married wealth several times before to assist.
- Finds files, videos connected to surveillance cameras set all around the house
- Some of the women appear to be in a dungeon
- Freaks out
- She picks up the phone to call police … he answers. But the phones only ever call inside the chateau, my dear. He catches her (of course)
- Takes her to throw her in the dungeon

- The videos were not live – all the women are dead
- But she's carrying the letter opener she had given him for a wedding present (she had made it herself)
- She stabs him in the eye
- She escapes, he follows, and when she reaches the top of the tower, she has a choice to make, be captive or leap.
- She leaps. As she hits the steel grey water, her breath is driven from her body and, rising above the sea spray, is carried way on the breeze.

······

I begin writing according to my plan. As I do so, I find the writing arriving organically. I deviate from the plan, following my inner impulse. Here is the result:

The laughing man

I should remember every detail of when we first met. After all, I was to marry the man soon afterwards. At the time, I believed it to be a chance encounter: we were simply in that place at the same time.

My attendance at the Summer Ball had been a last-minute opportunity: a ticket offered by a neighbour who had fallen ill earlier in the day. I was not prepared, but unwilling to let the occasion pass, I dressed in the only suitable garment I owned: a red satin dress I had made for a school assignment, my sewing teacher encouraging me to experiment with fit, feel and flow.

I felt beautiful in the dress, and yet was surprised to see so many heads turn to look at me. A 'slip of a thing', is how people usually described me. And young, so young. But my smallness and lightness meant that I was a natural at climbing, a hobby I had kept hidden from my conventional parents.

As I walked about, I noticed the other young attendees wore white, but the evening was not one for worries: I was at the Ball.

Dresses and coat tails swirled past me in blurs, the air was alive with music, voice and laughter. Liveried staff appeared out of nowhere holding silver trays of Marie Antoinette champagne glasses on the tips of their fingers. Dare I take a glass?

Before I had time to reach out my hand, he appeared, the man who would become my husband. He held out a glass to me and smiled as he watched me take a sip. My first taste of champagne.

I recall it being bitter, dull and heavy, not the sparkling wisps of enchantment I had imagined champagne to be.

The vibrant evening fell away until there was no-one else there but the man. Him, and a woman who appeared constantly behind him, nattering in his ear. The chime of midnight signalled my return home, and as he helped me into the taxi, my companion promised that we would meet again soon.

That night, my dreams continued the spell of the evening. In them, I danced with a handsome man who guided my every step. My dancing partner was tall, with broad shoulders, a strong jaw, full lips and a deep voice. And when I awoke, I imagined myself in love.

The next day, I was summoned to my father's ready room to find a man there who acted as though he knew me. He was of medium build and height, with thin, badly cut hair, a scrawny face, ill-fitting clothes, and red patches of peeling skin above eyebrows that almost met in the middle.

'My child,' my father began, as that is how he addressed me before guests.

'Have you promised your hand to this man?'

At first, I couldn't respond, so surprised was I by the question. The man was closer in age to my father than myself. I did not recognise him, nor did I remember meeting him.

'No, father,' I replied, for that was the truth.

'Your daughter, Sir, is perhaps playing hard to get. She spent the entire evening with me at the ball and sealed her promise with a kiss.'

'Did you kiss this man?' asked my father.

Recalling that I had drunk champagne last night, I feared I may have forgotten the moment. But surely not. How would I be able to forget my first kiss?

'Perhaps your daughter is ashamed of admitting she spent the evening in the company of one man,' prompted the visitor. 'I have brought with me my sister, who can vouch for your daughter's promise.'

At that moment a woman appeared, as if from nowhere, but most likely she had been sitting quietly in the bay window awaiting her invitation to speak.

'I confirm that this girl is the one who promised to marry my brother,' she trilled in the high-pitched voice of a bird.

'And I saw her kiss him of her own accord.'

Before I could open my mouth to protest, my father spoke. 'So be it, then.'

He clapped his hands loudly and the room was immediately filled with busy servants, for there was a wedding to be arranged.

That was several months ago, and now I am fully sequestered in another house, now my home, and can never return to that from whence I came. The rules my father set are never reversed.

'You have made your bed, now lie in it,' he told me as he gave me away at the wedding, the only impact my tears made being on my white gown, not his heart. Why not turn to my mother, you ask? My mother is so without substance that she may as well not exist. Appealing to her would have been to appeal to my dog, powerless as they both are.

Now, in this place I must forever call home, I am cut off from all that I knew. No friends call on me, and I may not contact them myself, no, cannot contact them myself, as all my attempts are intercepted, and all means have been removed. I am constrained to stay within the house and forced to lean far out of the window to feel the touch of the sun upon my skin.

How can I stand this life, you might ask, and the answer is, I cannot. I must try to escape. I should try, but then, I have nowhere to go. My husband took the generous dowry bestowed by my father, and it was immediately paid towards his debts. I did have an account of my own, with money earned by hard work on weekends and holidays, but he took that too, yelling, and ranting and raving at me, running up to the walls and raking his hands over the surface like a demented creature, tearing his hair and showing me the fine strands in his scrawny hands. I would have done anything to stop the madness and so I gave him my access details. The account is now empty.

As the days pass, my will to leave dissipates. I find that hours and sometimes entire days pass by, and I with no memory of them. I feel nauseated, my head hurts, and my physical strength has left me. Each night, and many days, he forces me to drink some vile liquid he says is wine, but I know is not, as once, when I was trying to push the cup away, it spilled, and a green the intensity of fluorescence spilled onto the floor.

It is always after drinking this liquid that my memory fails me.

One day, he did not return home. It had been half a day since I had drunk the vile liquid and strength was rising from my core into my limbs. He had never left me alone for long, and I hoped, oh, how I hoped, that he had befallen some accident, perhaps a fatal one, and would never return.

Trembling, for fear was never far from me, I ran to his office but the door, of course, was locked.

The room next to it had a large window, and I looked out of it to that of the office. They were not so far apart, not so far as to make reaching the one from the other impossible, and before I was given up into this bondage, I was school climbing champion. I looked down to the rocky slope several stories below and wondered if I should give up before I began.

But the mood was upon me. I knew I may never again have such an opportunity. I climbed into the open window and stood within its frame, turning to face the room. I stretched out my left leg towards the ledge of the other window. First my toes and then the ball of my foot, but I hesitated there, my body trembling more than I could ever believe possible. I heard a harsh rasping noise: it was my breathing. I decided I would pull back but before I could act, my weight was transferring to my left foot, habit formed from years of training, and I was straddling the two window ledges. I was nearly there. The window easily opened, then I was on the floor, barefoot, standing in his office.

The room was as I expected: a large desk occupied much

of the space. The phone was there, and I should have been reaching for it, but instead, I was mesmerised by the collection of items on the desk.

They all belonged to me. My diary, my pen, my favourite book, some of my underwear, my watch, my grandmother's pearl necklace, and the letter opener in the form of a miniature sword, a gift from my favourite Uncle, his souvenir of Toledo. I picked it up and turned it about in my hand. I loved the efficiency it once lent to opening letters, cleanly slicing through the top.

There was also a large button set atop a box. I could not resist. I reached out and pressed it.

The wall peeled away exposing rows of monitors. They were video surveillance. Could it be? It was. The cameras were set throughout the house, in every room. I understood, now, how he always knew my every move, arriving from nowhere to scratch my every itch.

I should have been reaching for the phone, but I could not draw myself away from the monitors. And then, there he was, on one of the screens. He was waving at the camera, smiling directly at it, as if he knew I could see him.

With a whoosh the office door flew open, and my husband stood in the doorway, laughing. Chin high, hands on hips, he laughed and laughed and laughed.

I kept the desk between him and me, standing with my back to the window. I could feel the fresh air lifting my hair and hear the chortling of a magpie on the breeze. I longed to be out there, outside, away from here.

'You're quite the star!' said my husband, picking up a remote control from a little table close to the door.

He turned towards the monitors and the images changed to the same view. I couldn't believe what was before me.

The video was of me. I was stumbling about, as if drunk, and my husband was there, laughing, pushing me into positions and forcing his body into mine. The fleshy white moles across his back reflected with sweat in the obscenely bright lighting. The realisation that he'd been drugging me and forcing me to have sex made my stomach shrink into a small, hard lump of cement.

Watching my face with pure glee, the fiend pressed another button, and the channel changed. This time, each monitor played a different video. No, not different, but variations on the same theme. There was me crying, there was me, eyes unfocussed, being dragged by the hair, there was me, hands tied to a frame, and in every scene there was he, poking, prodding, pushing, shoving, crowing at the camera.

I screamed, and as my husband watched me, he laughed. He laughed and laughed and laughed. He pressed another button and a door on the far side of the room opened. I could see from where I was that it held equipment the likes of which I had never seen in real life, equipment used for bondage.

'Get in there. Now!' ordered my husband, no longer laughing.

I did not move. I was scared. Scared of what defying him would result in. Scared of what obeying him would mean.

He moved to a cabinet and extracted a bottle. Pouring what I knew was the vile liquid into a glass, he moved towards me.

'Here's some wine. You like wine, don't you?' He said in a kindly tone, as if he were not a monster about to drug me.

My resistance was seeping away. I felt so weak, as if the

blood was draining from my body. What was the point of trying to escape, I thought, remembering my father's words.

I have made my bed, now I must lie in it.

As I took one final breath before submitting, hot tears started pouring down my face.

He began to laugh again. Loudly, violently, the sound buffeting my ears, rousing my wits, and the more he laughed the more my fear melted away. I became angry. My anger grew into fury, rising from my gut and moving into my chest, the lump of cement liquefying into magma. I felt heat flow along my arms, filling them with strength. I could feel the expression on my face change, the tight skin, relax. I stared at the monster with such hatred that I fear, for one moment, the devil herself had entered me.

My husband ran at me and as he did, I realised I was still holding the letter opener from the desktop. My lovely little imitation sword.

I stepped forward and thrust, the blade barely piercing his stomach. It did not kill him, of course it did not kill him, but it stemmed his attack. He started to bellow and fell against the window frame, wailing and moaning like he was the star of a second-rate melodrama.

I stood back and watched him, watched him wail. And by the time I had called the police, he had fallen from the window, and onto the rocks below.

He had begged me to help him, and help him I did, and in doing so, I helped myself.

Later, when speaking to the police, I stated that as I was phoning for help, he had fallen from the window. Who would believe this slip of a thing could have tipped him up and over the window ledge? But I did. I watched the ground rise up to meet him and continued to watch for minutes afterwards, afraid that he would stand up and return to the house. And come for me. But he never moved again.

There would be nothing to inherit, no longer a roof over my head, as my dead husband had never really owned anything, but had borrowed, embezzled and stolen money which he lost, always lost, crooked piece of work that he was.

I had to leave before the monster's family came, for they would never let me go. The documents in my husband's office revealed the nature of their fortune – they were pimps, and were they to lay hands on me, I would remain forever a slave in one of their dungeons.

I packed a bag with my personal items and walked to the nearest train station. Before falling from the window, the bundle of cash the monster always carried about in his shirt pocket, the cash he used to impress people, had slipped out onto the floor. With that cash, I can buy a ticket to somewhere. I don't know where I am heading, but I depart with a lighter heart. From now on, I have my freedom.

Discussion

When I wrote the initial version of this story, I did so in one sitting. After a week or so of reflection, I returned to the story and altered the second half. I had originally followed closely the story of 'Bluebeard', incorporating a room of ghastly corpses, the remains of the previous wives. On reflection, I realised the husband in my tale would not murder a valuable asset, his personal sex slave. I amended the story to suit the aspects of intimate partner abuse I wanted to expose: manipulation, control, sexual and financial abuse. The horror lies not in a chamber of corpses, but in the revelation of the extent of the abuse experienced by the wife.

In the various versions of 'Bluebeard', the wife is rescued. In the original, it is by her brothers; in Angela Carter's version, by a gun-wielding mother. In both versions, the wife accepts the verdict of death delivered by her husband and while she hopes for rescue, she is resigned to her fate. Not once does she name the husband for the multiple murderer that he is. I wanted to create an empowered victim, one who is not rescued but who saves herself. One who, accustomed to submitting, almost does, but is saved by an innate sense of self-worth, determination and courage that manifest previously in a subtle act of disobedience against her parents: participating in rock climbing at school. It is in recognising her innate sense of self that she is able to drive the blade into the monster.

Disobedience of a single rule is the focus of Perrault's 'Bluebeard'. This is clearly borrowing from the Bible, where Eve disobeys the single rule imposed by God, to not eat the fruit of a specified tree.[4] 'Bluebeard' has other parallels with Genesis: Bluebeard is not present when the act of disobedience occurs and yet he knows it has occurred. The sense of being under someone's control even when they are not present is representative of a victim's loss of agency in long-term abusive situations.

The moral of 'Bluebeard', as with many other such tales, is that the punishment of the wife is brought on herself through her act of disobedience. Marina Warner, in her discussion of 'Bluebeard', notes that publications of the story that followed Perrault's often have subtitles such as 'The effect of female curiosity'.[5] This 17th century blaming of the victim continues today: I have experienced it firsthand, and I have heard highly educated women make statements such as, 'They must have been brought up that way' as justification for the suffering of domestic abuse victims. I also have heard many times, 'She must have done something to deserve it'. And that perverted comment, 'It takes two to tango'. As if being abused is a dance in which the victim is a willing participant. Those are 'morals' I do not want to perpetuate. In my own act of defiance, I changed the emphasis from an act of disobedience to an act of self-determination.

I reflect on the significance of being rescued. So many fairy tales I know, Snow White and Cinderella come to mind, end in the victim being rescued by a handsome prince. I consider my own life in the context of research revealing how women exposed to domestic violence in childhood are more likely to experience it in adult life.[6]

If this is the case, a woman trapped in an abusive relationship may find that a male rescuer appears to offer her a better life. But in the case of serial victims, for those indoctrinated at a young age, the new situation may replicate the former abuse or degenerate into something worse. This I know from my own lived experience. For this reason, my protagonist needed to change, to act with courage despite her fear, and to rescue herself. I am pleased with this story.

Reflections

On reviewing this chapter, I am reminded of the role played by scenes of brutality in fairy tales. In 'Bluebeard', for example, the chamber holding the remains of Bluebeard's wives forces us 'to pay attention to a very serious message'.[1]

In Perrault's version, the wife understands the message and submits to her fate, as does the wife in Carter's version, after quickly assessing, then dismissing, her chances of escape. In the story I wrote, the protagonist is confronted with video evidence demonstrating sexual brutality. Yet, it is only when faced with further debauchment that she takes a drastic step in her own defence.

I wonder why there must be an impetus too gross to ignore to jolt the protagonist into realisation? It is here that the true story of domestic abuse is to be found. This female has been indoctrinated since birth in abuse that switched off her innate desire for self-preservation. There were no alternate role models provided by care givers. She is unable see her situation as an external observer would.

For me, there is something unfathomable in the metamorphosis from victim to victor seen in my protagonist. How is a person, indoctrinated from birth in her domestic abuse roles, to step into another way of being?

I see much of myself in this story; yet the strong, courageous action taken by the young woman to venture into the world alone, severing the ties which were chains constricting her, that action is the fictive work of my older imaginative self. As a young woman, I could have no more walked away from my life of domestic abuse than I could have changed the colour of my eyes. Judith Herman describes this as a state of 'psychological domination'.[2]

I genuinely believed that my life was as it should be, that the good outweighed the bad. I had no compass with which to seek another direction. This way of making sense of one's own life, is fixed; it is as integral to the self as one's own genes. Change is possible only with the ability to step outside of oneself and to observe one's own life from a distance. While my protagonist did not have any external assistance, this is only a fairy tale. In real life, we need genuine intervention: reliable support, role models we relate to, people who help us set out on new paths, people who become our new family.

HORROR

Writing what cannot be spoken

CHAPTER 9 WHISPERS

EXPERIMENT 8 (APRIL 2018)
REFLECTIONS

I set 'Testimony' (Chapter 7) in a cafe, where conversations are not private. This left me thinking about situations where people overhear details and expressions of emotion that were once relegated to the home, office, or telephone box. The private, the personal, the confidential, these are all making their way into spaces that jeopardise these categories. The man who lives across the road turns his doorstep into a megaphone, projecting his voice into the neighbourhood; a driver uses her car speaker system to publicise the contents of her phone conversation. On the train, a woman tells a 'secret', someone else's secret, over the phone. 'Don't tell anyone!' she warns. Is it a secret if a dozen strangers have heard it? We are all potential eavesdroppers, even if we only hear one side of the conversation.

The type of text I would like to create is inspired by advertising. I have seen advertisements where the people are not speaking but captions show their thoughts. I would like to write a piece that reflects various thoughts and occurrences as held by a range of people in a common space. I ask myself if my narrator sees inside people's minds, or does she overhear snippets of conversations?

I decide on a location, and start writing, seeing where this will take me. Here is the result.

Magistrates court

The whole situation here is sordid. I walk into the forecourt from the street. Journalists and photographers are lurking outside the building.

> *Is that them?*
> *Is that him?*
> *Is that someone?*

Cigarettes thrown to the ground; urgency turns to movement.

> *Quick, they're coming! Get the shot!*

A young female journalist dressed in ridiculously high-heeled shoes and ultra-mini skirt, and her cameraman, brush past me, descending on a couple not far behind me.

I keep moving, even more disconcerted than a moment ago.

A 'once-friend' steps out from behind a column. A camera, almost too large for his tiny body to hold, is poised on his shoulder.

> *Oh, no, it's her.*

He breaks off eye contact and tries to step behind the post, but I've called his name. He doesn't respond and instead, looks past me. I follow his gaze. There's the rapist, the reason I'm here today, the man my camera-toting once-friend decided to call 'friend' although they were never friends before.

'Can't talk, working,' he whispers without moving his lips.

I don't want ... to see me talking to her.

It was some time before I'd learnt that he'd betrayed our friendship for a dodgy mortgage deal arranged by the rapist. Dodgy mortgages were his thing. He simply manufactured pay slips from his parents' family trust that showed high earnings for the client, and he raked in the payoff for securing a mortgage. The ex-friend and his wife now have a holiday home they couldn't have obtained a loan for otherwise.

Thank God, she's gone.

I feel his relief brush against me like a puff of putrid exhaust fumes.

Shaking, I try to get through security before the rapist gets close to me. Everyone's in a hurry to get through.

Which floor's it on?
Have I got everything I need this time?
Bet the bastard doesn't turn up again.

I line up with the kindly-looking elderly security guard, but the surly one waves me over. He goes through my bag slowly, holding up all the items for all and sundry to see. I nervously try to make small talk, but he ignores me, and starts chatting with the next person in line before he's finished with me.

I'm not getting into trouble for chatting with the females again.

It takes forever to gather up my belongings. I dash into the ladies' room and wait for a long time before I attempt to take the lift. I'm still shaking; my skin is clammy. I try drinking some water but choke. My throat is little more than a lumpy mass, and I cannot swallow.

I share the lift with a heavy smoker who reeks of chemical compounds. His mind is certainly elsewhere.

Bitch is gonna pay for this.

I head past men of all ages. Some are sitting on benches that line the walls, others are standing. They are grey, washed out.

Gonna really give her something to complain about next time.
Can't believe it's come to this. I barely touched her.

I try not to look directly at any of them.

A young man, surely still in his teens, is moving in circles, agitation dripping from him like sweat.

Fuck, fuck, fuck!

I head directly for the safe room but am refused entry. I'm told that I am the perpetrator, that I have to sit outside with all the others in that category.

'But I'm the victim,' I tell the guard through the sliding glass window.

That's what you all say.

'You're not on the list,' I'm told.

I look over and see the rapist pretending to cry, talking to a social worker. He's pointing at me, he's making a scene, moaning and wailing about being scared. I feel his eyes burn into me.

I always win.

After Magistrate's Court this morning, I have to appear

in another court, across the road, the Supreme Court, with that same vile louse. In that court he will also play the victim, begging the judge to award him my home, my investment properties and my future earnings. In all cases I am treated by the judges as immoral, corrupt and criminal. My argument that the rapist is using the court system maliciously to intimidate me is always dismissed. And outside the court, the vile creature laughs at me, hugely, hands on hips, mouth wide open like a clown head in side-show alley.

But I refuse to let him win.

Just across from me, there's a man leaning with his face against the wall. He looks so sad.

> *No-one believes me. What am I going to do?*

While I'm waiting for the female staff member to become available to assess my worthiness to enter the safe room, I hide myself away from the louse, but still within view of the security guard.

> *Just sit there where I can see you.*

I see a man sitting quietly, looking down at his lap. Is he a perpetrator? He looks harmless enough. Oh, God, did I just think that? Violence isn't worn like a mask. Maybe his situation was a once off.

> *Why did I have that extra drink the other night? I never lose my temper. Why did I choose that time to confront her about her Internet affair? Why did it all get so out of hand? Why? Why? Why?*

I'm distressed I'm not allowed in the safe room. It's unimaginable that I have to wait in the same space as the louse who raped me, who is still stalking me, all because the legal system allows him to take protection orders out against me.

I look up and see a man staring at me. What's he thinking? That he might try it on? That I look like his wife, sister, mother? That he might follow me afterwards and hit me across the head from behind?

What the hell's she looking at?

I approach the guard at the safe room, repeating my request to be allowed to wait inside.

Not her again.

I go to return to my seat and realise the rapist has moved into it. He's staring at me with everything, his eyes, his head, his shoulders, his hips. It's confronting, as if a weapon is aimed at me.

You want a piece of this, don't you? Women love this. Say 'pretty please' and I'll visit you again. I know how to get in, don't you forget it.

I stand so close to the security guard that he asks me to move away. Eventually a social worker comes out to speak with me.

Haven't you been here before?

She checks some paperwork and confirms with the staff that I was in the very same safe room just a week before. Finally, entry into the 'safe' room.

Inside, there is a hyped-up woman with dark bruising on her neck, speaking with the social worker. I say hyped up, because her voice is loud, her speech is rapid, and she can't keep still. She's insisting that her case is next: she has to get back to work. There's something I can't put my finger on. She's heavily made up, and her dress sense suggests she is probably younger than her face looks. I guess that she's a heavy smoker, and her jitteriness is caused by a need for nicotine, but once we've entered the safe room, if we leave, we cannot return.

God, I need a smoke.

When it's my turn for the social worker, the other woman makes a poor show of pretending not to listen in. I really don't like that, the way that some people make no effort to allow you privacy, taking pleasure in other's suffering. I lower my voice but the eavesdropper leans in closer.

Here's something juicy for the girls back at the office.

The social worker leaves me to speak with a young mother who looks so very tired.

Where are we going to sleep tonight?

My name is called and just in time, my solicitor arrives, her strong presence making her appear even larger than her stature alone. I'm the only one in this room that has representation.

I wish I'd gotten a solicitor. She must have money.

When I walk into the miniature room that is the magistrates court, the judge doesn't look at me. When he does cast an eye over me, his face is dripping with disdain.

More of the same.

I stand and listen to the rapist crying loudly, begging the magistrate to make me stop scaring him.

Tsk, tsk, chatters the magistrate.

It's my solicitor's turn to speak. She stands up and thrusts out her chest and starts strutting, just like the male barristers hired by the rapist's family for criminal court. I half expect a crest to rise up on her head, like my Muscovy drake when he's angry. I'm disgusted at the stupid, childish games that pass as normal behaviour in the court system.

The magistrate intervenes.

'Ms B….., I hardly believe it is necessary for the respondent to have legal representation.'

The rapist's hands drop from his face. He stares gleefully at me.

Oh, this is too good. You've played right into my hands.

My solicitor points out that the 'man' has been charged with rape.

'Accused! Accused!' whines the rapist.

'Charged. And he has had over a dozen cases of stalking reported against him.'

'Stop!' The magistrate does not speak, he bellows.

My solicitor is not allowed to continue. That information belongs in the criminal court, not the magistrates court. Here, it is inadmissible. The magistrate will only consider the complaint before him, the one claiming that this 48kg woman has been threatening the poor, crying man who is standing there, grin hidden behind his hands.

This is stunning!

It's inconceivable that a magistrate with as much experience as this one must have, given his age, can believe such an act. Yet he clearly does.

THE WRITING PROJECT

> *There's no smoke without fire. She can pretend to be innocent all she wants, but she's done something, or she wouldn't be here.*

The magistrate berates me, and out of the corner of my eye I see a grin on the face no longer pretending to hide behind the hands.

Ha ha ha ha ha haaaaaa.

Discussion

I found this writing practice revivifying. The searching for ways to express repressed emotions, to unravel cruelties born of a court system that perpetuates victim abuse, the attributing of thoughts to a range of characters. Within the realms of this stimulating writing practice, it was if the words flowed through my fingers to appear on the screen of their own accord.

A few days ago, I began to write a story with no connection to my topic, my experience, or true life.

I had found, quite by accident, a very small book, a 'Penguin Specials', as I was leaving my local library. The book is 56 pages long (approximately 12,500 words). It is a quick read. I added it to my loans and read it on the train on Wednesday. That night, I began creating my own 'Specials' novel. I wrote it for the joy of writing. It is the writing, the creative expression, that is pleasurable, so much so that at times it was difficult to draw myself away.

I am enjoying reading, now, too.

My approach to overcoming block, these writing experiments, is working. Writing for my own pleasure, for my own benefit, is becoming familiar again.

Reflections

Looking back over this chapter, I note how the style I used aligned with what I needed to express. That heuristic approach to writing mirrors how I used to write before block. This represented a growing shift away from block to greater expressive freedom. I believe freedom of expression is important to creativity, especially when attempting to portray the complicated situations, scenarios, emotions, and events that stem from living with domestic abuse.

Sophie Tamas speaks of the difficulty of writing about her experience of domestic abuse within a single genre, which she finds restricts and limits the complicated truth she wants to communicate.[1] With hindsight, I recognise the interrogation that a victim of violence receives in court as a well-established genre. As with all genres, there are rules to follow. In a courtroom interrogation, the defence barrister plays a role, one of his own choosing, where he struts and yells, lunges and falls backwards in mock horror, mimicking a maniacal rooster; the interogatee, the key witness and victim, is an unwilling role player, forced into a one-size-fits-all costume that is too tight around the ribs, inhibiting her breath. It is also too long, so that she trips, stumbles and falls. What she says is controlled by the genre enforcers, the defence, the police prosecutor, by the deals made between them on behalf of the man on trial. The jury are one-dimensional, all of them together, a single erasable slate, wiped clean as soon as the witness has breached her confines, saying more than she is allowed.

I am with Sophie Tamas. We need our voices to match our words,[2] to be unapologetic if we make strange sounds as we speak, to combine words that do not combine, to conjugate words that are otherwise conjugated, to use our language to communicate the depth, the complexity, the embodied truth of our experience. To break the rules of every genre if we need to. If we can write in ways that enable rather than disable us, writing then, becomes our ally, our companion, our true voice.

WHISPERS

Writing away the powerlessness

CHAPTER 10 DIARY ENTRIES

Experiment 9 (May 2018)
Reflections

Libraries are magical places. They offer the adventure of new knowledge, or the means to 'travel' to other realms. They are a sanctuary, the walls of books cushioning patrons from the outside world. They are places to study, research, read and write.

    I love the physical act of seeking suitable books, walking amongst the aisles, perusing the shelves. Sometimes I do this slowly, examining every spine in a section; other times I merely scan, trying to squeeze just a moment more of searching into time that will not wait. What am I searching for? Sometimes I have no clear idea. I survey the titles for the glint of a precious jewel, a sparkle of light, a reflection of potential brilliance. And perhaps a sign. I reach out and draw such a book from the shelf, weigh it in my hands, glance over the blurb, perhaps the contents page, and sometimes I read a morsel. Mostly the books are returned to the shelf. But not always. Occasionally I grasp the book to me, concerned it will be removed from me by the person browsing the shelves nearby; sometimes I slide it under the books I have already chosen, hiding it from view, or nudge it into my bulging book bag. And sometimes I stand there reading, obstructing others. In this way I found myself holding, reading, lost in another of Helen Garner's books, *The Feel of Steel*,[1] specifically, the section called 'Tower diary'. This is a collection of short observations. The style of this work of nonfiction inspires this chapter and my next writing exploration.

It is the beauty in her vision which draws me to Garner's writing, the way she conveys this in her descriptions. In this book, she shares moments of her life as she adjusts to her changed circumstances. She notices beauty, suggesting that it seeks her out. It is this positive, affirming approach to life[2] that I hope to capture in my writing for this piece.

Diary

Front row centre seats for the Queensland Ballet. The friend I subscribe with insists on these seats where we crane our necks to see the dancers. At times we only see those who stand immediately above us. She likes to see the expressions on their faces. As do I, but without their sweat dripping on me, please.

The performance takes me by the arms, swirling me around the stage. Afterwards, I float my way to the car, still under the spell of the story so convincingly conveyed by those arms, those legs, those bodies, those expressive faces.

My friend is insisting we saw the same performance earlier in the year, with most of the same dancers. I deny. She insists. Is it possible to have forgotten? And yet, it is true. I have become so numb from the trauma encompassing my everyday life that when I do have the opportunity to escape, I do so utterly. I do not remember that first performance, as I do not remember most of those I have seen in the past few years. Perhaps I should save the money of my subscription tickets, and, and what? These moments of bliss should be treasured for what they offer me: a couple of hours of respite from the constant guillotining of my soul that awaits me outside the enchantment of the performances.

…

Another weekday, meaning another day to deal with court matters. I join the queue and file yet another document. Will this one go missing, too? Anyone can sign out a court file, run their eyes over the sordid details of the participants, make surreptitious copies with their phone, slip out originals of documents and steal them. I want copies and pay for the privilege in both dollars and time. I must return after this date, after this time, to collect them. Draw a queue number, wait amongst those being paid to be there, and those, such as myself, who are self-representing. I leave, resigned to return soon. No not resigned, less than that. Condemned.

…

No, no, I don't think I can stand anymore. My chest is imploding, my bowels are twisted, my vision is blurred. On my doorstep lies a card, handwritten by the rapist, and a gift. Over twenty such breaches of bail so far, and so far, no action by the police. He makes a mockery of the bail conditions: the police make a mockery of the law. Do I bother wasting another two to three hours at the police station to make a statement? Do I risk being insulted by the police yet again? They want pictures of him breaching bail, but security cameras are still prohibitively expensive. Within the next decade they will become affordable almost overnight, and I'll outfit my house with them. But for now, they are out of my reach.

…

One of the students at the university gives me a gift: a diamante brooch. She's not my student, or one of those I have provided academic assistance to. But she has seen me helping others, chatting with those looking sad, or sick, and she wants to do something for me. I wear that brooch so often, it eventually falls apart. I keep the pieces in a box with my other broken mementos. Some of the pieces are all I have of past loves.

…

The moments just before dawn are mine. I stand at the window and listen to the first birds of the day: today, it's the crows; yesterday, the kookaburras. The rising sun throws her arm in my direction, sending out streamers the colour of cockatiel cheeks and crests. The cool air begins to warm and the sound of traffic increases. My ducks call out to me, so I rush downstairs to let them out, but I am always too slow. One of them has railed so forcefully against her enclosure that her beak is bleeding; another has leapt onto the wire door and is hanging by her claws. I assist their exodus and they move past me, waddling in line, huffing and squeaking their way to the food. My day must begin now and will not end until I collapse on the sofa, hours after my morning companions have gone to sleep.

…

Shock at what I face when I attend court today. The judge throws out my submission because, somewhere in the past, my solicitor spelled my name wrong. The rapist is unable to contain his glee and laughs like a lunatic. He doesn't stop, despite the reprimand from the judge.

…

I wake up screaming, as I do every night. There's someone trying to force open the bedroom door, and I am trembling so hard that my teeth crash together. A voice, my partner's, home for a short time only, away for work more than he is at home. He yells at me for locking him out, for screaming. I let him in but feel no comfort in his company. I lie stiffly in bed as he begins to snore, the burdens of my life roaring loudly in my ears.

...

I have a hearing test and learn the tinnitus I have suffered since I was attacked is permanent and will only become worse.

...

We go away for a night, my partner and I. We walk on the beach in the dark and shine our torches on hundreds of tiny ghost crabs, busy with their own affairs. The wet sand is cool underfoot, but the water is warm. Despite the humid summer night, we cuddle in a single sleeping bag, hiding from mosquitoes. I am tiny in my partner's arms, and despite sleeping out in the open, I feel safer than I have for a very long time.

...

I have another court appearance. Another. This time I take a group of supportive women, an entourage that lends me strength. Why don't you write about it, one of them asks? Why don't I indeed? It is not until later, once the constant pressure of being stalked, being sued, being harassed by police, by the associates of the rapist and his family, that I realise I have lost my ability to write. To write about the wrongs would be to name them, thus depriving them of their power. It will be over a decade until I find my creative self again.

...

I'm preparing lessons for my classes. I reach into one of my bookcases at home to pull out a reference book and a copy of *Alice's Adventures in Wonderland* falls into my hands. There are several of them, hidden throughout the house. They are tiny reminders of lost childhood dreams and tiny reminders of hope.

...

Meet me for lunch, says a friend. I have little interest but agree. I have not yet completely lost my desire to socialise. We end up at a jumble of stalls and pop-up shops – an attempt at revitalising a desolate space that once housed a major department store. Despite my strong objections, I end up seated at the table of a fortune teller. It seems my friend has other people she wants to catch up with. She won't accept that I can entertain myself for a while. The 'fortune-teller' has made some little effort to look the part, the turban being that little effort. But her demeanour, language and behaviour convey a complete lack of conviction in the part. I'm too polite to get up and walk away, so I sit as the woman takes card after card from a pack and asks me, do you know a Pisces? do you know a Virgo? do you know a …? My words cannot convey the boredom in her voice and her actions. Think monotone, think impatient flick of the cards onto the table. I try not to stare at the face more rubber than skin and flesh. My responses, always negative, inspire anger. Don't you have any friends, she spews, the venom in her voice matched by the look of, could it be hatred? on her face. I have no idea about people's star signs, I explain, but she is not listening. Another woman has arrived with a plate of food and with that in front of her, the 'fortune telling' is over. I hesitate, debating my options.

Should I just walk away without paying? What exactly am I paying for? Should I tell her what I think of her? She's a bulky woman, rough, and my friend is nowhere in sight. The hand in my face demanding payment decides the matter. I hand over the cash and walk away, the woman so face-deep in the food that she wouldn't have known if I'd gone or not. So, tell me all about it, says the cheerful voice accompanying the arm that is threading through mine, but before I can begin, my friend is talking about people I don't know, spreading gossip like a communicable disease.

...

Another busy day. I almost miss the messages of love emanating from my adoring dogs. They are generators of love. When I do stop to take it in, I feel so glad that, despite everything, I have managed to keep our home, and us, together.

...

I attend an enormous, multicultural wedding. At the table I'm placed at, I make conversation with the woman next to me. She is a kindergarten teacher. When she learns I'm an academic, she turns hostile, the pretty face growing red and blotchy, the body language becoming stiff, uptight.

'I know someone who works in ... Department, I'll check if she knows you,' she states, twice, before turning her back on me.

I let this unsettling interaction worry me for some time. The way forward would be to develop a thicker skin. But I can't, and don't, because that's not me, and I don't know how.

...

The rapist is suing me for my home, investment property, household contents, shares, superannuation, his legal fees for

DIARY ENTRIES

the rape defence and $100,000 cash. Why that sum, is anyone's guess. His father calls me on my landline. It will all go away, he tells me, if I refuse to give evidence in the rape trial.

...

A day that looks like any other, except it is not. There are no courts to attend and no classes to teach. Not even any marking to do. We go hiking and, for a time, I forget about my burdens. On the trail there are goannas, young ones, that spring away into the undergrowth or claw their way up the trunk of the nearest tree. I feel guilt at disturbing their slumber in the sun. A bejewelled bug has hitched a ride on the rim of my hat, hanging upside down in front of my face. Hello! I leave it where it is. Eventually we reach its stop, and it flies off. How many little creatures use me as a form of transport on the walk?

...

My partner is home from another training exercise. Determined to catch the stalker in action, he hides in the front yard. Unfortunately, the person he catches is the junk-mail deliverer, who I see crossing the street from my home from then onwards: he never again delivers at night. My partner waits until sunrise: he's a solider, and can sit still all night, on the alert. The next morning, we check the mailbox and there it is, the latest delivery from the stalker. He'd been there earlier in the evening, while my partner and I were catching up after his extended time away. I'm sickened to think that he could have been, would have been, watching us through the chinks in the bedroom windows. If only we'd delayed our lovemaking to the next day, my partner might have caught him. But he didn't catch him, and even when we do supply photographic evidence of his being close to my house, within the 200 metres specified in the bail conditions, the police accept his excuse – he didn't realise where he was. Seriously? 'Charming' is how the detectives describe him, describe the rapist, stalker, thief, assailant, fraudster. Charming.

...

The postie squeals past on his nasty, 2-stroke bike. I collect the envelopes he has thrown on the ground and take them inside. In one is a credit card with my name on it, from a bank I've never dealt with. It will be years until I stop receiving new credit cards with my name on them, applied for by the rapist. The banks aren't interested in the truth: they tell me to destroy them if I don't want them. Never mind that a man has forged my signature, fraudulently used my details. Why would he do that? people ask me, disbelieving, meaning, I'm making it up. The insidiousness of intimidation, infiltrating my life like smoke through cracks in a wall.

...

I consider myself fortunate to have good support people. I have a counsellor, a spiritual healer, and my doctor, the one giving evidence at the trial. One after another they each tell me the rapist has been to see them, gaining appointments under false pretences, then revealing his intentions. They all tell me that he cried, begging them to see how sincere he is in his love for me, begging them to stop supporting me as a witness in the rape trial. Not one of them reports it to the police: all leave it up to me to do so. As always, the police accept his excuses: he didn't know she was my counsellor, didn't know he was my spiritual healer, just chose any doctor at the clinic. Is there no space in my life where I can be free of that deviant?

…

I pay the locksmith and he leaves. $120. The second time in two weeks, and I feel no safer. The rapist persuaded my homestay student, a teenage girl who arrived in the country yesterday, to give him her key. The police eventually ask him to leave but do not charge him. I find clothes that aren't mine in my wardrobe – a small pile of men's T-shirts, all of them white, and brand new. I take my entourage of loving but defenceless dogs to another room and lock us all in, furniture pressed against the inside of the door.

…

Security at work have a photograph of the rapist and assure me they will escort him off campus if they see him. Unlike the police, they take my safety seriously. My supervisor keeps an eye on me as I park in a spot she can see from her office window. Later in the day I collapse, and she takes me to the medical centre, where the force with which I project vomit makes us both laugh.

…

My homestay student tells me the rapist climbed through the bathroom window, found her where she was hiding, under the covers in her bed, and demanded a key. She's only 16, and she's tiny, so tiny. I don't hold blame against her. Oh, but if only she had told the police the truth.

….

He won't come back, say the police. Shows how little they know. Or care. He does come back, daily, nightly. Bit by bit, the tools are stolen from my garden shed. Regularly, the power is turned off, the water. He sends around his friends and associates. Just tell them to go away, say the police, but that's not the point, is it? Intimidation takes many forms, and that deviant has an unending supply.

...

I receive a letter from the rapist's solicitor expressing his client's concern about all the calls I'm missing without my phone. His client is kindly allowing me to collect it from his office. The phone he stole from me the night he broke into my home, assaulted and raped me. The phone he used to send messages to all my contacts on the same night telling them that I was insane, a liar, a sexual pervert. The phone he has been using to receive calls meant for me. The phone he has had in his possession for close to six months. I add the letter to the others. I'm becoming so immune to these multifarious attempts at intimidation that this one barely registers.

Discussion

The pieces in Helen Garner's 'Tower diary' that inspired me are short, sparse, and almost minimalist, requiring the reader to fill in the missing information. When writing my pieces, I aimed at replicating this style. I assumed, as diary entries, that the pieces printed were the entries as originally written. Now that I have attempted to write in this style, I realise that Garner's pieces have most likely been reworked before being published. When I wrote my own pieces, I tried to write them as if they were original diary entries, but the reality is that I would write, then revisit and rework the pieces. It was difficult keeping them short: the writing was flowing and there was much to say, so I wrote first and returned later with pruning shears and a focus on brevity. The result is a collection of pieces that present some aspects of some events, but there is much more, perhaps I could call it substance, that has been omitted. I wonder, if a diary is memoir, if omitting some details impacts on the truth?

For example, the piece about the locksmith and key originally provided more detail, showing the involvement of other people and relating the physical response I had at being unable to create a place of safety in my home.

> A phone call from a neighbour: the man is in my house.
>
> I call the police and abandon my class, driving home to find the rapist demonstrating his door-unlocking skills to the police.
>
> They accuse me of wasting police time and tell me it's a domestic issue, to sort it out with, with that man? He laughs and tells them I'm insane, that I'm an alcoholic.
>
> They look at me, at my crying face, my madly shaking body, and nod.
>
> I try to prove he doesn't live here. I take them into my bedroom to show them that it is the room of a woman, and there, on one of the shelves in my walk-in-robe, is a small stack of freshly ironed, new-looking white T-shirts. Men's T-shirts. And hanging on the rack are men's trousers in dry-cleaning plastic wrap.
>
> Right then, I do feel I am insane.
>
> I don't know how to make this insanity end. How can I get him out of my house if the police believe he belongs there?
>
> I find the receipt for the locksmith: the locks were changed again just last week. I give the police the number of the woman who was with me at the time, urge them to call her and call the locksmith.

The police officer asks my homestay student if she gave the key to the man. She quietly says no. She has only just arrived, and here is a man at least three times her size, in a uniform, asking her questions. She must be terrified. I can tell that the police officer wants to believe me. He looks at the receipt, calls the locksmith.

He then asks the man to show him his key. He compares it to mine. His is not numbered and bronze like the rest of them; his is shiny and silver. The officer confiscates it and tells the man to leave.

I know there will be more than one copy of the key, and the locksmith is at my home, again, within a couple of hours. Another $120 gone, and I feel no safer than before.

······

While the original version contains more information, it is too long for the style I wish to use. Consequently, I deleted details to create the final version.

Writing for an audience, and not only for the self, means working with the chosen genre(s) to create a text designed to be read. This involves engaging with the format of the text, its structures, utilising language to achieve certain effects, and making choices regarding inclusions, omissions, chronology and time. If a writer were to set down everything that occurred in a period in her life so as not to make any omissions, the piece could never be completed. It would contain every movement, every thought, every word uttered, every car that drove past, every sound heard, every smell.

I think about being in the witness stand in criminal court, and being questioned on the most minute of details, such as how many times did my head hit the floor when I was being assaulted? How many seconds was it from the moment I opened the door to the moment my hair was being pulled? How long did it take until my head hit the floor? These minuscule details were being played with by the defence in an attempt to prove I was lying.

And yet, I was forced to withhold other details, although they did occur, as the defence had negotiated with the police prosecution for those details to remain unknown to the jury.

I was not allowed to say the rapist had tried to sexually assault me previously and had forced me to engage in sexual acts under duress. I was not allowed to say that he had restraining orders placed on him by other women. I was not allowed to say that his business partner, waiting outside the courtroom, body slammed me as I entered the court. Where is the truth in that? Truth, even in the court system, is an element to be manipulated.

So, when it comes to life-writing and memoir, there are decisions to be made. The pieces above presented as 'diary entries' were not entered as such in a diary. They did not occur in succession; many days and weeks have been omitted. They do not include every detail, nor mention the players' real names.

One team of researchers, in examining the notion of truth and writing, ask the question, 'If we intentionally choose to not reveal elements of an experience, are we accurate?'[3]

Well, of course not. It does not mean that we are lying, either. One way to avoid the conundrum surrounding truth is to present writing as fiction instead of memoir. Significantly, what we write for public consumption is controlled by a legal system that protects perpetrators of crime. For this reason, it is often necessary to change names and other identifying details such as dates or place names.

Through this writing experiment, I was able to experience a greater sense of generosity in my writing praxis, enjoying the process of playing with a style while remaining true to the stories I wish to share. Emulating Garner's style was the conduit for engaging successfully in the creative writing process. Part of this success stemmed from a connection with Garner's style; part of it from my ever-growing desire to write. The theme of domestic violence is found here as the aftermath of a violent event, the impetus for a new story of ongoing abuse. The style I used offered the opportunity to set out some of the mundane issues that wove in and out of my life, contributing to and compounding the trauma I was experiencing.

Reflections

These short pieces provide glimpses into the flimsiness of a woman's safety when she is not taken seriously by society, by those in positions of authority, by those around her.

Light is reflected onto the ingrained beliefs within our society as regards blame, and the deeply held practice of denying a woman's reality by questioning the veracity of her concerns. The police telling a victim of violence that 'he won't come back' when there is evidence that 'he' will and does. The immediate rejection of one's truth in saying, 'but why would he do that?' Marilyn French, in *The War Against Women*, says, 'the real attitudes of a society often lie buried from view, and can be extricated only by close analysis of behaviour, language, and images'.[1] Writing, such as the diary entries above, allows the documentation of some of the many concerns that are ignored, that remain otherwise unrecorded. Until the minor details, the many mundanities, the cumulative ignorables that snowball into an overwhelming sense of threat, are documented and acknowledged, the 'close analysis of behaviour' remains slanted toward the grand, the newsworthy.

Why does it take a high-profile murder before there is public outrage? I ask you to consider the case of Rosie Batty, whose son was murdered by his father in a public space in 2014. I wonder if this murder, manhunt and subsequent shooting of the perpetrator by the police were not conducted in public spaces, would Rosie Batty have received the same media support for her campaigns to raise awareness of domestic abuse issues?

I compare her case to the violent death of Sandra Peniamina in 2016, who was stabbed 29 times THEN bludgeoned in the head with a chunk of concrete. This occurred in front of her son. Her husband was charged not with murder, but with manslaughter. It is recorded that he 'killed his wife in the heat of passion caused by a sudden provocative act'.² Had this murder taken place in the public domain, in a crowded shopping centre, for example, Sandra Peniamina's plight would have taken on a different value. Her vulnerability, her inability to stand up for herself after the first, the second, the 29th stabbing would have been clear to all.

Rosie Batty survived her son. With incredible courage and strength, she founded a public campaign against domestic abuse. Sandra Peniamina lost her life; her dreams and her future contributions have been lost with her. There is no person making a stand for this loss. And of the other women in Australia, more than 40 killed this year, every year, in what is so inaptly labelled 'domestic violence'?

We all have full lives. We are busy, keep ourselves busy. It would be impossible to take up every cause that we agree with. It is easy to say, well, this person, this organisation, is looking after that cause. I hear that. all. the. time. However, for fundamental change to take place in a culture, it needs to occur in the individual, the family, the community and in every element of society and its institutions, including, but not limited to, legislation and policies. Change from the bottom up, and the top down. We need to see it and live it, making it as natural as not throwing our rubbish out the windows or defecating on the pavement as people pass us by.³

So natural, that it need only be brought to light when there is aberrant behaviour. This makes the challenge of eradicating violence against women and children an enormous responsibility for associations created by individuals and small groups. The few taking on what must be the responsibility of every individual in our society.

DIARY ENTRIES

Writing my truth

Chapter 11 L'écriture féminine

Experiment 10 (June-July 2018)
Reflections

Along this writing journey, I have witnessed my own realisations about the mind/body connection to trauma, and its impact on expression and creativity. At this point, I can confidently say I have broken through the complete block that was my starting point. With effort and persistence, riding out many setbacks but always returning to my resolve, I have been able to reconnect with this form of self-expression, thereby regaining an important part of myself. In doing so, I have learnt about the integral role the body holds in responding to, processing, and maintaining the impact of trauma.

However, while I am in the process of regaining my writing self, my physical body is failing. I now live with a chronic illness that succeeded where the man who tried to destroy me failed: it deprives me of living the life I loved. A life of hiking, movement and adventure, a life of independence, travel and endless possibilities. I agree that 'given the ease with which health infuses life with meaning and purpose, it is shocking how swiftly illness steals away those certainties.'[1]

Regaining my ability to write creatively will help me, does

help me, to adjust, adapt and accept. Without the structure and accountability of this research project, I would not have embarked on this journey of experimentation, attempts, and gradual gains. To be in the reduced physical state I am now in, and not have writing to turn to, would have seen me as a hollow self, trapped in a weak body where 'time unused and only endured still vanishes, as if time itself is starving'.[2]

I am full of gratitude for the success of these writing experiments. I now embrace each moment of this project as an adventure, excited at the prospect of further cultivating my writing practice. Writing will be my means, my journey and my destination: if my body denies me adventures, I'll create them. I think of Elisabeth Tova Bailey, author of *The Sound of a Wild Snail Eating*.[3] She, too, lost her health as a consequence of a viral infection. She, too, drew on her writing self to transcend the restrictions of her illness.

L'écriture féminine is about writing the woman. It is more than writing from a feminine perspective; it is writing from the female body. My body, this failing body, this body that remembers health and yearns to thrive.

Hélène Cixous wrote in *The Laugh of the Medusa*, 'Write yourself. Your body must be heard. Only then will the immense resources of the unconscious spring forth.'[4] In preparation for this section, I read powerful samples of this type of writing: A.S. Byatt's, 'Body art', and 'A stone woman'.

Reading has an important counterpart in writing, a point I emphasised when teaching. I found that some students persisted in the unsuccessful approach of practising writing without reading and studying good models. When I wrote in the past, I was doing so with a strong foundation provided by a corpus of classic literature. I had read, and studied, what I was taught to think of as 'The Greats': writers from The United Kingdom, Ireland, France, Canada, The United States and Australia. Having studied the Bible at school facilitated my understanding and analysis of many of these works. I also read many critical works as I explored the original texts, which led me to read other works that influenced, or were influenced by, the text being studied. I thus studied the novels of D.H. Lawrence, which led me to find Henry Miller and consequently, Anaïs Nin. My readings included poetry, plays and prose. When I reached for my pen and writing material, my hand was moved not only by own thoughts, responses, queries, expressions of emotion, but also by the strength imparted by the texts I had read.

When I lost my writing self, I lost not only the ability to write creatively, but to read and engage with anything other than texts for transactional or work purposes. When I eventually regained the ability to read creative works, it was limited to nonfiction. Through these, I tried to satisfy my fundamental desire for adventure, although at that time it was more escapism, reading memoirs written by women who stepped out of the bounds of the mundane. Books such as *Down the Nile: Alone in a Fisherman's Skiff*,[5] *Sinning across Spain: A Walker's Journey from Granada to Galicia*,[6] and *The Bookshop that Floated Away*.[7] In these books I found solace, the opportunity to witness another's journey, to experience other perspectives. However, my reading of these books was not in an imaginative, picturing myself in the authors' shoes, living vicariously, way: it was as if watching the story on TV. There was a barrier, a field of interference, caused by blocked creativity. I lacked the imagination to fall into step with the authors of those adventures.

Now, however, that interference has greatly diminished. I am reading more, and I am also starting to enjoy fiction as I once did.[8]

Reading 'A stone woman' left me thinking about change, particularly how our bodies transform at different stages in life, and how those of us who are traumatised often lose a natural connection with our bodies. This led to thoughts on denial, and being denied, of femininity. I know from my own experience that I have spent years covering my body from others, in public at least: an attempt to prevent uninvited, overtly expressed interest. Sarah Ahmed says of this type of unwanted intrusion on our female bodies:

> You begin to feel a pressure, this relentless assault on the senses; a body in touch with a world can become a body that fears the touch of a world. The world is experienced as sensory intrusion. It is too much.[9]

Over the years I was involved in indoor climbing, I developed a heightened sense of this pressure. I attempted to create a barrier against the unwanted intrusion, using 'clothing to reduce the visible markers of womanhood.'[10] I wore baggy trousers and t-shirts, the sleeves covering my shoulders. How foolish I was to think my dress code would protect me from unwanted words, uninvited actions. Instead, I was regularly teased, and sometimes mocked, for dressing this way, by males and females alike.

On the few occasions I did wear a singlet or sports pants, I was assaulted with comments on my figure by both males and females. I felt bruised, dirty. I was told by my belayer (the person in charge of keeping you alive by managing your rope), 'I like watching your bum'. My female climbing companion happily pointed out male interest: 'You should wear those more often,' she encouraged. Once, twice, older men reached out unwelcome hands, pulling my top away from my body to expose my breasts. Laughing when I objected. These unwanted, unacceptable actions weighed heavily on my sense of self, on my feeling of physical sanctity.

My current body context relates to a health condition that has impacted on how I live. This illness has not kept me safe from tyrannical male behaviour. I have learnt NOT to accept offers of assistance from older married men who speak of their wives and children in the same breath as propositioning me. That awful term, 'fair game' comes to mind. Now, I set aside the constraints of my illness to see myself as growing into a new form, as a woman in metamorphosis: mind and spirit evolving. I am learning to live with a body that behaves differently to before. I am learning, slowly, to work with, and not rail against, these changes. I want my writing to express this sense of metamorphosis, to express prior denials and impositions, to express transformation, to suggest future promise.

Considering these aims, and influenced by 'A stone woman', I feel no need for brainstorming of ideas, planning, or any other preparation for writing. Instead, I write. My aim is to see what arises. Without a solid idea for a story line, yet able to draw on creative impulse and a writing exemplar, diving into the writing process is allowing ideas to surface. Here is the result:

Leslie

Leslie's earliest memory of his father is the only memory of his father. It's not one he has ever spoken about, not one that he ever will. He has it stored away in a safe place, one his mother will never find, the way she found the mummified mouse he'd hidden in his room. He'd thought the small carved, wooden box, secreted below the floorboards under his bed, was safe, but his mother found it all the same. He'd gotten home from school, had a school chum with him, when his mother dangled the tiny form in front of his face, and began rebuking him in her native dialect. The school chum, Jack, Joe, something like that, made a quick get-away, but Leslie didn't have that option, wouldn't have run out on his mother, anyway.

Another town, another house, another school. Leslie never knew where he would be the next day. His mother cropped his hair close to his scalp, pulled the thick vest over his arms and head, forcing it over his chest. It was tight. At first it was hard to breathe, but Leslie soon got used to it.

'Breathe from here,' his mother told him, touching his belly, 'breathe and speak from here.'

On their holidays in the mountains, Leslie had run around in loose garments, free from any kind of restriction. He'd discovered he could sing in quite a high voice, pitching it from the rocky outcrops. It was just him, the rocks, the wind and the wary birds. But now it was back to behaving in a civilised way, and Leslie conformed to expectations. Few words, low voice, and playing football. No more singing or dancing about in his grandmother's old nightgown.

The night Leslie's mother died he'd been out with his school chums. He didn't really like that scene, the pub scene, drinking and looking girls up and down, but he went along with it, because that was what was expected of him. He'd never been close to a girl, not because he didn't like them, he liked them a lot, but not in the way they wanted him to. Leslie didn't want to take their knickers down or see their breasts; he wanted to spend time with them, talk, gossip even. He preferred them to his chums.

The priest made the arrangements; Leslie followed in a daze. His mother had always been there, had protected him, guided him, moulded him. He was now his own person. Or alone. Either way, he was free.

Later, long after the service had ended, and the air had turned cold, Leslie returned to the church. He sat thoughtfully, watching the burning candles melt. Entranced by the melting wax, he fingered the creamy globules with tenderness, longing to know how the wax felt as it transformed, from solid to liquid to solid again, never looking the same as when it began.

The night of his mother's burial, Leslie opened the secret box in which he kept the memory of his father. Again, Leslie was a four-year-old. It had been a long night: the screaming had gone on, and on, but it had stopped. That's why Leslie had gotten out of bed. He'd needed to pee for hours but was too scared to leave that safe space. It was finally quiet, so he slipped out of his room and tiptoed along the corridor. There was a light on in the kitchen, so he crept to the door and peeked around the frame. His mother was sitting at the table, her face in her hands. Her left hand, the one Leslie could see, was dirty-looking, black and purple and swollen. On the floor was a man. Leslie could see his legs twitching, hear him making gurgling noises, like the time Leslie played at drowning in the town pool. Then a voice, a name. Martha, Martha. It came from the man on the floor. Leslie's mother rose from her chair. He could see her face clearly, but it was wrong, all wrong. The colours, the bleeding, the swellings.

His mother picked up the iron frypan, the one that was too heavy for Leslie to lift, and swinging it above her head with both hands, drove it down towards the ground. Leslie saw the man's legs spasm and then the twitching stopped. There was no more gurgling noise, only the sound of his own breath, and the sound of his mother sobbing.

…

The day after his mother's funeral, Leslie visited the little shop in the foyer of the church, buying dozens of candles. He liked the tall, thick ones best, but they only had a few of those, so he also bought short squat ones, and tall, tapered ones. Leslie packed them all into his mother's car. He was heading to his grandmother's old farmhouse. It was a long drive into the mountains, but Leslie had all the time in the world. He stopped a couple of times to walk across the rough landscape, to climb the rocky outcrops that increased in number the closer he got to his destination. He unfastened his vest, the one he never took off, and drew in a torso full of air and sang. It had been a long time since he had heard that voice, that light, high voice, and he laughed to know it came from him.

That night, the fireplace ablaze, Leslie took his time setting out the candles. He placed them on the mantlepiece, on the floor, on the tabletop, on a stack of books that rose up to chest height. He put on his grandmother's old nightdress and stepped lightly across the floor. He lit the candles, one by one, and as he did so, he addressed each one, as if a guest at a party. Surrounded by the flickering, Leslie closed his eyes and imagined his past melting away. He imagined himself as a little girl, playing with dolls and wearing dresses, he imagined going to the birthday parties held by the girls at school, choosing frocks with his mother, brushing his long, curly hair.

Leslie fell asleep dreaming these dreams. He imagined the flames in the fireplace grew to join the flames of the candles.

He imagined that he was a giant candle melting, melting. He imagined his grandmother's nightdress exploding in flames, exposing the flesh of a young woman.

Laughing, Leslie leapt up from the floor and tore the nightdress away. By the candlelight he saw what had always been denied. Leslie opened the door and ran out into the safe, inviting darkness, her breasts bouncing freely, her thighs rubbing together, tickled by her pubic hair, and raised her voice to the wind.

Discussion

In *The Body Keeps the Score*,[11] Besser van der Kolk presents examples of patients who, as a result of trauma, have denied connection with their bodies. I was taught by my mother to deny the debilitating pain of dysmenorrhea. She told me it was my duty to bear it, that I had no right to complain. And certainly there was to be no pain relief. The first time I was offered pain relief was in my final year of high school. I was on the point of fainting. My teacher, a nun, assisted me. She expressed surprise that I hadn't told her I was in pain. She gave me my first panadol.

Until then, I was denied acknowledgement of menstruation, made to believe it was shameful. Likewise, the protagonist in the story was denied her gender by a mother who wanted to protect her from men. Through this exploratory writing, I have found a way to right a wrong, to speak from the truth of the body, acknowledging what is being denied, by the self or by others. In it, there is celebration of the body just as it is, free from external impositions.

If 'female writing means allowing each individual to write her own unique story,'[12] then when adopted into writing for the self, it can play a powerful role in gaining agency through acknowledging and celebrating one's own body.

Reflections

Whether we acknowledge it or not, the female body is often repressed. Even when we write (tell stories, paint, sing, perform), calling attention to our 'different biographies of violence',[1] we are accused of feeding a culture that thrives on women's discomfort, pain and fear. Leslie Jamison refers to this as fetishism of female suffering.[2]

To support and nourish us, to help us find ways of living with the experiences that compromise the sanctity of our bodies, Sara Ahmed proposes compiling a survival kit.[3] As a former hiker, I recognise the significance of a survival kit. Instead of containing a bandage and iodine, thermal blanket, matches and aspirin, this kit contains a manifesto of non-negotiable personal beliefs and rights. It also holds favourite readings offering us strength and companionship, serving as a means of remembering and connecting with others.

In writing about my experiences and acknowledging writing as an embodied act, I have been enacting a form of defiance, a transgression[4] against the tyrannies I have experienced. Speaking out and speaking up can be too dangerous for those within a domestic violence context. For those of us who have found safety, we can use writing to generate a shared experience, gifting strength and a sense of connection. This is a potential life belt for others to cling to when they are prevented from making those external connections in any other way.

Through reading Ahmed's book, I was introduced to an online space that serves as a venue for sharing one's own experience of the unwanted, demeaning acts committed against women and girls. This website is a place of solidarity, a place where women and girls can freely share their experiences. While this sharing space is not limited to domestic contexts, the sexist acts committed against women and girls is deeply connected with the abuse that occurs within families and intimate relationships. I have added this website to my survival toolkit: https://everydaysexism.com

THE WRITING PROJECT

Writing into freedom

Chapter 12 Writing as Strategy

Experiment 11 (August 2018)
Extemporaneous writing
Reflections

As my ability to read and engage with fiction returns, so too has my desire to expand my reading repertoire. I have thus (finally) encountered J.M. Coetzee and Gabriel Garcia Marquez. While I had intended to explore magical realism for this experiment, I found myself being drawn to just start writing. This is the creativity inside me pouring out without the restrictions of a pre-fixed genre. This is how I begin:

> No, Mummy, nooooo!
> With a loud snap, the mother flipped the book shut and stood up.
> Stop that right now, young lady.
> Her voice, as usual, was no nonsense.
> But Mummy, I don't want Charlotte to die.
> For God's sake, Amanda, it's only a story. If you're going to carry on like this, I won't read you any more stories at bedtime. Understand?
> The mother hesitated at the door, finger on the light switch.
> Understand?

> The little girl blinked away her tears and cuddled her teddy. Yes, Mummy, she said softly.
>
> That night, Amanda dreamt of reading the story herself. She was holding the book in her hands, reading the words out loud. Before her eyes, the words turned fluid, rose from the page and rearranged themselves. She heard her voice as it spoke the story, only, it wasn't the same story as her mother had read to her. It had a new ending, a better ending, a happier ending, just like in the fairy tales - happily ever after.

......

These words flowed from within, without preparation. This is how my writing practice used to be: erupting, scripting itself on whatever scrap of paper was at hand. The shape of a written piece grew from the stimulus: a passionate encounter could result in a biblical-influenced piece of eroticism (think Old Testament), or a daydream that slightly oversteps reality. I used my words to spin tales that entertained me, that entertained the wicked in me. At times to write was therapeutic; at others, it was intellectual; and at still others, it was pure escapism. In all cases, it played a significant role in my life.

My writing is now more spontaneous. Would you agree that I no longer need these writing experiments, that the block has been replaced by at-will writing? Consequently, this chapter represents an end to the experiments. As I complete this aspect of my research, I see myself turning to the collation of the chapters into a coherent, complete work. This means writing other elements to contextualise, introduce and finalise the entire project. These will include writing an Introduction and a Conclusion. I look forward to this next step with trepidation, as it, too, will be a learning experience.

For now, I return to my writing exploration for this chapter. I have in mind a protagonist who is the antithesis of a fatalist. She believes that the past can be changed. The little girl who refuses to accept that the spider dies in *Charlotte's Web*,[1] also will not accept the pain and disappointment in her life as fact. She writes into a sense of control, rewording events in her life, and eventually, in history. In this way, my protagonist successfully uses writing as a strategy to overcome life's difficulties. She does not follow the path carved out for her by her family, one of continuing abuse, humiliation, and subjugation of self. She does not grow into the serial domestic abuse victim prescribed by her family upbringing. Her writing allows her to carve out a new existence for herself. Firstly, this is as temporary escapes from the trauma of her childhood. Then as an adult, she makes her way in life using her writing to heal those beyond herself.

Inspiration for this writing exploration has come from novels I have recently encountered. With my renewed ability to read and enjoy fiction, I am discovering a plethora of authors previously out of my bounds. I actively engage with the act of reading, asking myself what makes the writing successful in my eyes. The eyes of a reader who would be writer. These books have included *Tin Man* by Sarah Winman,[2] whose compassionate exploration of the heart and soul of two characters allows the reader to become immersed in moments of great beauty, and to share in moments of extreme sadness. The unfolding of the events of the past result from moments of change in the life of the key protagonist, the one whose life continues when the life of the other has ceased. It is the reflection on the past, and the consideration of alternative futures, that reveal the magic in the actual moments lived. I take the idea of using a moment of change to inspire my current piece.

Another joy to experience was *The Map of Salt and Stars* by Jennifer Zeynab Joukhadar.[3] I felt the storytelling enter my eyes and pour through my body in a waterfall of enchantment. I found many elements in this novel engaging. There are the parallel stories. One involves the protagonist, a twelve-year old girl, Nour, and her dangerous journey as a person vulnerable to the events and people around her. The other story is a fairy tale told to Nour by her father. For Nour, this other story is living in her and with her, connecting her to her father after his death. Her family understand the importance of this story and at times, it forms a point of reference for discussion amongst them.

At times, the fairy tale is brought into the main story in exciting ways. Such as when Nour reaches out and takes hold of elements of this other story and brings them into her own life, not as a means of escapism, but as a way of helping her to make sense of her world. For Nour, then, this alternate story is a source of grounding for her knowledge and beliefs. There are familiar points of reference in the fairy tale that Nour is keenly aware of, such as the role of maps beyond simple identification of places. There are even times when Nour believes she can situate herself and her family in the landscapes they pass through based on the descriptions in the fairy tale. What I took from my reading of this book to use in my own piece, is the impact that colours can have on transforming a moment in time. For Nour, colour is another sense, like smell or sight. I will use colour as an element to build magic into a scene.

These books have left me with a desire to write something

new, something different. Perhaps, like the novels I have read lately, leaving the reader (which is me, and now you) with a sense of wonder, surprise, or bafflement. My ideas come to me in fragments: a snippet of a dialogue, a scene playing out in my mind, the images of the setting, the sounds, the feel. I write these down and later assemble them, eliminating repetition of ideas through the drafting process.

When I think of my protagonist, I imagine her story as occurring over a lifetime. However, a more concentrated time frame would better suit a short piece. To this end, I have been considering how best to create a more contained time frame or context. I have always been drawn to stories set within a 24-hour period. I think of *Who's Afraid of Virginia Woolf*, *The Rocky Horror Picture Show*, and some of the French arthouse films I watched as an undergraduate. And of course, *Alice's Adventures in Wonderland*. I think this may be one way to contain this potentially expansive storyline.

I wonder what other contexts I could use to limit the time and place of my story? With many ideas jostling for attention, I return to a technique discussed in an earlier chapter. This technique will help me to set out all those ideas, regardless of their usefulness, to gain clarity of thought. From there, I can plan a strategy to start writing.

THE WRITING PROJECT

Brainstorming Session

Topic: context (time and place)

Time: 5 minutes

Materials: blank sheet of A4 paper and a sharpened pencil

Result: The number of ideas I assembled was not large. I had hoped for more. However, through the ideas generated, I establish that the context will pivot on a moment of change. This change causes a shaking up of the past, a reawakening of memories. This change, this upheaval, is what allows the story to be told. I have decided to place this key to change towards the end of the story, to allow a more chronological presentation of the protagonist's life.

The girl who would rewrite history

'No, Mummy, nooooo!'

Snap!

The book shut on any possibility for discussion, for explanation, for helping a young mind grow.

The mother stormed towards the door: a force of repressed anger and frustration in a floral house dress.

'For God's sake, Amanda.'

'But Mummy, I don't want Charlotte to die.'

The mother hesitated in the doorway, finger on the light switch. She looked angry. She nearly always looked angry. Or tired.

'It's only a story,' she forced out between clenched teeth. 'I'm fed up with this. I'm sick and tired of you carrying on all the time. Anymore, and I'll send you to a psychiatrist.'

Amanda's mother stood up taller, puffed up by the power

she held over the child.

'And you know what he'll do to you, don't you?'

The little girl cuddled her teddy harder and blinked away her tears. Her mother had been threatening her with the psychiatrist for as long as she could remember.

'They put wires in your brain,' her mother had told her. 'Electrical wires.'

The psychiatrist was, to Amanda, more terrifying than any monster she could dream up.

She had to convince her mother she was a good girl. She took a deep breath and drew out the mask of composure she kept in her hidden box of happy things.

She looked up at her mother, tearless.

'Yes, Mummy,' she said softly.

That night, Amanda dreamt she was reading the story all by herself. She was holding the book in her hands, reading the words out loud. Before her eyes, the words turned fluid, rose from the page and rearranged themselves. She heard her voice as it spoke the story, only, it wasn't the same story as her mother had read to her. It had a new ending, a better ending, a happier ending, just like in the fairy tales - happily ever after.

...

In the past, libraries were quiet places. Makers of noise were hushed, readers looked up when disturbed by the scraping of chair legs, a cough, or the shuffle of a heavy walker. Otherwise, the sounds carried were of the soft, papery kind: pages of books being turned, abrasion of pencil across a lined page. Today, public libraries are community hubs, hosting play groups for children, and loud conversations. Comfy chairs have been replaced with computer stools positioned awkwardly at monitors. People are coming, going, drinking coffee, eating food, chatting on their phones, yelling at their children. It is more cacophony than peace. Quiet reflection is long gone.

Except, of course, in the ancient libraries, the ones sustained within the protective embrace of the oldest of the universities. Like the one where Amanda was on sabbatical. She had visited it years before when investigating the possibilities, the options, for her plans. This library was absolute perfection during the day. Visiting scholars were required to check in their electronic gadgets at the desk and access to most areas were by appointment only. Only a small group of general visitors were permitted in the main area each day. Amanda would watch them as they gazed about with great gaping mouths. She would look at these people, laypeople is how she thought of them, and imagine a stream of coloured words flying from the texts and into those empty caverns.

Most of the time the library was one of serious research. It was treated respectfully, reverently, as the treasure that it was.

Amanda knew the library was most alive at night, however, when the day's visitors had departed, and the doors were securely locked. During the day, researchers, visitors and staff exhaled fragments of their own lives into the air, these fragments settling along the tops of shelved books and on the pages of those open on display. At night, the books were the ones exhaling, the foreign elements having transpired into something new, something renewed. At night, the atmosphere in the library became filled with dates, names, formulas and poetry, with tales, facts and revisions of facts. And lies. Lost dialects and ancient languages intermingled, gathering in clouds so substantial they broached on being tangible. The components of the building itself, the panelled walls, the parquetry floors with their woven wool runners, the shelves, the railings and the tabletops, all exuded elements of the information captured by the texts.

Some might imagine that the library air would be toxic, but Amanda knew better. She thrived on the energy that almost crackled as she moved about.

Amanda entered the restricted area. This part of the library held the most ancient and valuable of texts, those reserved for the hands of select scholars. She understood the privilege of being allowed access to such a sacred space. Here the atmosphere was more concentrated than elsewhere in the library. As she stated her intention in a hushed voice, the air vibrated with anticipation. Amanda moved slowly along the aisles, left hand stretched out, not quite brushing the spines of the irreplaceable texts as she passed. The item she had selected to repair was a manuscript from the 13th century. Her sabbatical to the library was for only six months, and Amanda had accepted that she would not have time to work on all of the books. She had spent the first month reviewing the choices before selecting this one, a single manuscript yet to be reproduced or studied by modern scholars. This made it the perfect choice.

During the day Amanda worked on routine as well as specialist repairs to the texts in the library. This allowed her to source an almost exact match for the paper in the manuscript without raising suspicion. Replicating the calligraphy was the real challenge. She had successfully arranged for the analysis of the inks using Raman spectroscopy. With her connections, a fabricated research request was simple enough to produce.

But the reality was that certain ingredients in the inks were not available in the modern era. The likelihood that someone would authenticate the ink, though, sometime in the future, was beyond her considerations. She couldn't control what happened to the texts that she amended. She wasn't their guardians. Her role was to right wrongs.

The repair of this manuscript, specifically, the replacement of a single page, had posed many challenges, yet Amanda never faltered in pursuing her goal. And tonight, all her skilful efforts were to be made manifest.

Amanda donned her surgeon's kit: gloves, hair net, face mask, and smock. She had no intention of contaminating the vital essences of the text with her own modern DNA.

Amanda removed the heavy manuscript to her worktable. With confident hands, she revealed the spine. She glided the protector under the offending page, lined up the guide, and slowly, so slowly, sliced along the paper. She slipped the diseased page into a protective envelope and placed it to the side. Over the next two hours, Amanda affixed the corrected page to the spine of the manuscript with care and skill. It would take another expert to detect any tampering. The closest comparison would be the Vinland Map, a work that Amanda held in high esteem. It was not only the beauty of the map that she admired, but the purity of the intention underlying its fabrication.

Amanda carefully applied rehydrated glue collected in minute samples from other texts from the same era, and fibres from parts of the manuscript's spine. As she worked, ribbons of coloured words wound around her hands and forearms, spreading out into the room, a symphony of medieval colour.

Not once during those hours did Amanda's thoughts wander from the space she was in. She was a master at work, a magician performing her most amazing act, a healer bringing peace to a suffering world.

In her youth, Amanda had read about the suffering inflicted on people by others. Avoidable suffering. In a world where accidents, sickness and natural disasters caused so much pain, it was unfathomable that people would also cause suffering to others. And mass cruelty? Sieges, deprivations, enslavements, slaughters, genocide? In her eyes, these were the evidence of Satan walking the earth. Her response made her vow to right those wrongs she could, so that readers in the future, people who had once been children, just as she once was a girl, would not be faced with such horror.

While outsiders may have seen that Amanda did not have a happy life growing up, this was not how Amanda recorded her life. The diary she kept from the age of six reflected a portrait of love, support, encouragement, happiness. This reimagined home life gave Amanda the strength to push through when her sleep was disturbed by the droning voice of a man whose rage was unquenchable, the times when she made mistakes and received, not explanations, but a man's backhand across her face, or worse, the thrashings that were always preceded by a session of mental torture. At those times, the thrashing, whilst physically painful, was at least a sign that the emotional torment was temporarily at an end. Amanda didn't want to dwell on the humiliation she was forced to endure, being made to beg, squirm and thank her abuser, who would alternate between smiles and looks of fury. Instead, Amanda drew into being a family life of beauty and grace.

As morning drew near, Amanda replaced the completed manuscript on the shelf. She gathered together the tools that were her assistants in this important procedure, smiling, happily smiling, at the changes to the world that her repairs had created.

...

The old woman dropped the book onto the pile in front of her. It slipped to the floor.

'You alright, Mrs Cravens?' asked the girl with the messy hair.

The woman looked over at the girl.

'Who are you again?' she asked, her voice wavering slightly.

The girl sighed.

'I'm Britney. I'm here to help you pack up.'

'Yes, of course, dear,' responded the woman with uncertainty. 'Where are you going?'

'I'm not going anywhere,' replied the girl, rolling her eyes. 'You're moving into The Home.'

The younger woman looked at the older woman and shook her head slowly. She found this type of work depressing, but it helped pay the bills while she looked for something better. She walked over to the fallen book and placed it the box destined for the charity shop. *Charlotte's Web*. She'd read that in primary school. Why would an old woman have that on her shelf?

She shrugged her shoulders.

It takes all types, she thought.

'Will you be right while I work in the bedroom, Mrs Cravens?' shouted the girl.

I'm not deaf, thought the older woman. I'm old, but I'm not deaf.

'Yes, dear,' she said in a voice that she hoped inspired confidence.

'Right, then, I'll see you soon.'

The girl left the room and the old woman sat down in her special armchair. For all the years she had lived in that house, her special armchair had sat facing the bookcase that filled an entire wall.

She surveyed her books, the ones still on the shelves. It would be the last time she would see them, the last time they would be in her care.

'You are going out into the world, now,' she said softly. 'I hope that others will see in you the potential that I did.'

She reached over to the book on the top of the box and caressed it in her hands.

'You were my first,' she said.

She opened the book to the final pages. There it was clear that the original pages had been replaced. While she didn't read the text, she did run her finger down the sheets with tenderness. As she did, a tear fell from her eye onto the paper, and she allowed it to stay there, before closing the book.

...

The girl carried the small box of items the old woman was permitted to keep into the little room which was to be her home until she died. The old woman was sitting on the bed, staring into space.

'Alright, Mrs Cravens?' she asked, although her shift was about to end, so she really didn't want a response.

She didn't bother repeating her enquiry. As she passed the shift manager on the stairs, the well-groomed woman smiled at her and thanked her.

...

Before leaving the old woman's house, the younger woman had dug around in the boxes of books.

She had slipped her hand down the side of the larger books and pulled one out.

'I'm sure my little sis will like this.'

She had placed the book in her bag and left.

One day, soon, a girl child will be reading that copy of *Charlotte's Web*. And when she does, she will read an ending the original author did not intend, an ending that won't make her cry. An ending imagined by another girl child many years before.

...

Amanda Cravens obediently ate the small meal presented to her on a tray. Obediently, she lay down and went to sleep. The tiny room was no larger than the one she had lived in during her first year at university. 'Cells' is how they'd referred to their rooms, all those years ago.

The next day, Amanda awoke to rays of sunshine pouring into her room. Outside, the Magpies were singing while their young were playing hop hop on the lawn.

'I love this time of year,' Amanda thought, humming a tune.

In her flowing silk pyjamas, she strode along the corridor to her sun-filled lounge room. She sat back in the armchair and surveyed her books, smiling. The titles on their spines shivered and glowed.

'Now, my little ones,' she said to them, 'where shall we begin work today?'

Discussion

There is so much more to the writing process than the scribing of words. Writing involves the generation of ideas, the planning of plot, scene, time frame, and scope. There are details which may or may not be significant, such as the choice of character and place names, the era in which the story is set, and the location. There is also the style to consider, what the discourse can lend to the meaning and interpretation of the story, and the genre. And of course, the writer's motivation. In some cases, writing also involves research, as with *The Map of Salt and Stars*, mentioned earlier. The author conducted historical research into the life of a person she then developed into the character in her fairy tale. For my own piece, I drew on my undergraduate studies in archaeological science for the details on pigment analysis of the medieval manuscript. These are just some of the elements that contribute to the writing of a piece.

I felt a tremendous sense of pleasure during the entire process involved in creating this piece. Firstly, parts of the story, and ideas for it, came to me as fragments. As the creative process progressed, these ideas united into a writing flow until I had produced enough for my purpose. Because of this fragmentary approach, I deleted a section during the piecing together of the parts, as it expressed ideas used more effectively in another section.

The writing aspect of the creative process for this piece worked like this: I jotted down ideas, words, sections, in any order, giving voice to the ideas as they came to me. I worked on the continuity and language once these were set down.

This creative process flowed into other areas of my life. It has ignited sparks for other pieces of writing, not so much in terms of measurable writing output, but in terms of imaginings. By this I mean the dreamative aspect of the creative process, the conjuring of wildly swirling colours, scents and sounds from the mundane: whirlwinds from specs of dust, cyclones out of a stray drop of rain on a sunny day, Kew Gardens out of the impromptu bunch of flowers presented to me by a stranger while out walking my dog.

My progress from the beginning of this project is immense: I am reconnected with some of my creative outlets, particularly my writing. I now draw on my writing as a strategy for making sense of, and coping with, what life sends my way. As a result of this long and fruitful journey that has been these writing experiments, I now step back in time to pick up the pieces where I left them.

There is a room in my house I alone know exists. In it is an enormous dresser, the kind that might once have been found in castles, but which have long since been burnt into ashes. I open a top drawer, the one that is slightly ajar. It glides open as smoothly as one used daily, not one that has been abandoned for years. I lift out the oversized envelope, the one that feels as smooth as silk. It is made of acid-proof paper, its purpose to keep safe the documents inside.

At my desk, the one facing the floor to ceiling glass windows that overlook the southern gardens of my estate, I carefully lift out the page that is from a medieval manuscript. As I look at the words, their letters stream together and rise into the air. I hear a tuneless humming and realise it comes from me. I laugh, and the words fall back to the page and reassemble. Not as they were but as I would have them. A new ending to an old story, and for me, a new beginning.

Just as a child outgrows the need for training wheels on a bike, this chapter confirms my readiness to shed the protective guidance of the structured experiments and move on to my own freer writing practice. I had been feeling a growing desire to push against the constraints of the experiments; this has now grown into a full rebellion. Even before starting this chapter, I wanted to say to you, 'I can do it myself, now'. While there is still so much to do for this research project, the experiments are over. From now, I plan to write as I desire, when I feel the need, for myself, and maybe, one day, for a wider audience, utilising my growing connection with my creative self, my inner voice and strength. I share the extemporaneous piece of writing that leapt from me with joy, a celebration of my now found/renewed/new writing practice.

THE WRITING PROJECT

Extemporaneous writing (August 2018)

Aunty Luticea woke up last Saturday morning and decided, 'Today is the day.'

Not that last Saturday was particularly different from any other day, apart from being a Saturday and the first day of the weekend. That made it different from a weekday when she would have risen at 7am exactly. On weekdays, Aunty Luticea eats a nutritious breakfast of bran cereal and skim milk, with half a sliced banana on it, or sometimes, if the bananas in the local supermarket are too green, too large, too damaged, or too expensive, three slices of tinned cling peaches in natural syrup. She prefers the natural syrup to the sugary type, but she sometimes relents and buys the other owing to the extortionate difference in price. She never varies from this routine, not even on the day she gave birth to her one and only child, 25 years earlier. On weekends, however, Aunty Luticea treats herself to a slice of extra thick fruit loaf, removing just one slice from the bag in the freezer, never two, and toasting it. Sometimes she spreads it with marmalade, sometimes with strawberry jam. This Saturday, though, Aunty Luticea spreads her slice of toast with blackberry jam from the jar given to her by the woman who came to her door a few weeks ago, the woman who spoke to her about 'her options'.

That had been a strange morning indeed. Aunty Luticea had just settled down to watch some daytime television after finishing her morning household chores and was none too pleased at being interrupted.

Well, who could this be, she'd said aloud, almost hoping

the person at the door would hear her and go away.

But the knocking persisted, and Aunty Luticea did the only thing that was reasonable in the situation: she answered the door.

Mrs Winters? asked the woman standing at her door.

Yes, was the distracted reply as Aunty Luticea eyed the woman from head to foot. Aunty Luticea thought she was one of the most elegant women she had ever seen, apart from royalty, of course.

I'm Julia Drews, said the woman in the Chanel suit, with a handbag that matched her shoes.

Aunty Luticea was still busy looking the woman over when she noticed that the woman was holding out her hand.

Aunty Luticea was not used to shaking hands, not being important enough to invite it. It was her husband who spoke on their behalf, who took care of any business. She never had anything to do with that side of things. Her domain was the home, and her job was taking care of it.

I'm from the women's shelter, Mrs Winters, said the woman, her voice so well modulated that Aunty Luticea felt she could listen to it all day. Well, not all day, of course, but for quite a while at least.

Can I come in?

Aunty Luticea, responding automatically to the request, found herself making tea for the elegant woman who was by then sitting in one of the chairs, her chair, in the lounge room.

Once tea was served and the niceties were dispensed with, the visitor came to the point. Or rather, she dropped the bombshell.

We have accommodation available for you.

Aunty Luticea didn't say anything for a while. She wasn't sure this woman was actually there for her. Perhaps there's another Mrs Winters in the street?

The woman leant forward and put her hand on Aunty Luticea's. She gently explained how her daughter, her only child, had been to see them several times. She'd procured her permanent accommodation in a safe house in another town.

But who will take care of the house, my husband, the dog? Aunty Luticea asked, almost giddy at the thought of not doing her chores.

The woman showed Aunty Luticea pictures.

You'll only have room for a few of your belongings: your clothes, personal items, and some mementos. And your daughter will take the dog, said the woman, looking around for the dog she knew must be there.

Oh, he's out the back, said Aunty Luticea distractedly. My husband won't abide by animals in the house.

Aunty Luticea had always felt this was an injustice. Just why couldn't their dogs come inside? Dog after dog, they always stayed outside, living half-lives, catching only glimpses of the people they loved, always wanting more. More attention, more time, more love. Rather like Aunty Luticea herself.

The woman just nodded and took dainty sips of her tea.

Aunty Luticea remembers signing some papers, which she said she read but didn't, as she wasn't at all sure about what was going on, and wondered really if she should be signing anything, suggesting she should perhaps run the documents past her husband.

Mrs Winters, your husband can't be allowed to find out about this. This is for your safety. We're going to help you start a new life.

Before she left, the woman handed Aunty Luticea a jar of blackberry jam made by the women at the shelter. It's made with love, she said, before stepping out of the front door and out of Aunty Luticea's day.

This was a couple of weeks ago, and although this Saturday wasn't any different from any other Saturday, she decided that it was the day. The day to do 'it'.

Once she'd finished her breakfast and cleaned up the kitchen, she walked around the lounge room and collected the empty beer bottles her husband had left there the night before. There was a puddle of beer on the best rug. Again. Aunty Luticea got down on her hands and knees to mop it up, though she didn't know why she should be concerned, if she was leaving.

I can't leave the house in a mess, she said out loud. I just couldn't live with myself.

Once she'd completed her morning chores, Aunty Luticea went into the room that once belonged to her only child. She gently sat on the bed. When did her daughter start telling her she should leave, she wondered? She couldn't remember. It just seemed to be the song she always sang.

Mum, you should leave.

Well, today I will, thought Aunty Luticea, looking around at the room she supposed she would never see again. Just as soon as I've finished tidying up the house.

Aunty Luticea vacuumed the carpets in the lounge room and the hall, and then the main bedroom, although she didn't usually do the vacuuming on the weekends. As she dusted the shelves and the ornaments, she wondered what chores she would have to do in the women's safe house.

In the master bedroom, she lifted a large suitcase, a wedding present from her parents, down from the top shelf of the walk-in robe. She placed it on the bed, noticing the thick layer of dust across the lid.

Oh, we can't be having that, can we? said Aunty Luticea to herself.

She left the room and returned with her cleaning kit: rubber gloves, a microfibre cloth, and two bowls of water. One for wetting with, one for rinsing in, chirped Aunty Luticea in the singsong tone her mother had taught her. She hummed a tune from her early 20s while she cleaned the suitcase. She took the cleaning items back to the kitchen and returned with a polishing cloth. Once the case was as dust-free and as shiny as an old suitcase could be, she decided she could finally open it, and open it she did. Inside, there was nothing but space. A large space inviting filling.

Ah, now, what to take, said Aunty Luticea in a voice that was far less sure than the voice that spoke about cleaning.

Aunty Luticea started with her underwear drawers, laying piles of garments out on the bed. Many of them she hadn't worn in decades.

This will never do, she said, and decided to sort out the garments. Now, I know using a system is best when sorting clothes, said Aunty Luticea.

On the shelves in the lounge room was Aunty Luticea's collection of home living magazines. She had hundreds of them, organised by magazine name and year, held upright in magazine holders. She'd started with one holder, and now had almost 30.

I know I saw an article on sorting clothing in one of these, she said.

She pulled one of the holders off the shelf and placed it on the coffee table. She was about to sit down in her armchair when she realised it was time for her morning tea.

What a good idea, she said aloud, as if someone had made a suggestion she agreed with.

Aunty Luticea went into the kitchen, filled the kettle with filtered water, and turned it on. I do hope there's filtered water at the women's shelter, she thought, knowing what a difference it makes to the taste of the tea.

She placed two scoops of tea into her favourite teapot, the one she was given on her twenty-first birthday by a good friend, one who knew quality bone china made for the best cup of tea. It didn't matter that the lid and spout had been broken, so cleverly did her daughter mend it that really, she could barely tell it had ever been broken.

You should leave him, her daughter had said to her, when she found her mother sitting at the table, crying over the broken tea pot.

Why don't you just leave?

Aunty Luticea set out a cup and saucer. She never used mugs for tea. Although she had amassed rather a collection of them over the years, mostly gifts from clueless people, and some of them were bone china, she preferred the taste of freshly brewed, loose leaf tea from a bone china cup and saucer. She often wondered about this, and once decided that it was a combination of the delicate cup handle, the evident fragility of the cup, and the ephemeral quality of drinking tea, the moment passing along with the tea, into the past. It was a lived moment, never captured, except in the possibility of future moments suggested by the presence of her beautiful tea pot.

Aunty Luticea took her tea tray, with the teapot, cup and saucer, and tiny jug of milk into the lounge room. She placed it on the coffee table next to her magazines and started looking through them. It was in this position she found herself an hour later, with an empty pot of tea and a strong desire to urinate.

As she walked to the bathroom, she noticed the clock in the hall above the stand. Half-past eleven.

My, where has the morning gone? wondered Aunty Luticea.

After washing her hands and tidying the towels on the rack, Aunty Luticea realised she hadn't washed her husband's clothes from the day before.

She gathered them up, put them in the washing machine, then headed to the kitchen to prepare lunch.

A cheese and tomato sandwich with a thin spread of relish was what she favoured for a light lunch, and all her lunches were light, except for the Sunday roast which her husband insisted on, even in the full heat of summer. But, as it was Saturday, Aunty Luticea had a sandwich, which she took back into the lounge room. She continued looking through the magazines, noting down the pages with ideas she could use.

...

Aunty Luticea looked up at the clock on the wall and realised the day had gone. Soon he would be home from work, and he would be surprised if his dinner wasn't on the table when he walked through the door. It was always on the table when he got home, Aunty Luticea made sure of that, keeping it warming in the oven once it was made, and quickly transferring it to the table when she heard her husband's noisy entrance.

Aunty Luticea remembered the suitcase on the bed. From her bedroom doorway, she could see the open suitcase, and the piles of underwear next to it. She sighed and walked over to the bed. Before she closed the case, she reached her hand into the internal pocket and drew out a slim leather folder. She ran her hand over it slowly, gently, before opening it. Inside was a photograph of her as a girl. She was dressed as Jeanne d'Arc, complete with mail tunic and sword.

I am the ruler of my destiny, said Aunty Luticea aloud, stating the line written under the photo.

She smiled at herself, at the confident person she once was, that she could be again. She replaced the folder in the internal pocket, but before shutting the suitcase, she counted out seven pairs of knickers from the closest pile to hand and placed them inside. She zipped up the case and, lifting it back onto the top shelf, whispered, I've made a start.

She put away the rest of her underwear and turned out the bedroom light. As she pulled out the pan to cook dinner, steak, it always had to be some kind of meat for him, she smiled again and said in a voice that she recognised from all those years ago: tomorrow is a new day.

Reflections

Clarissa Pinkola Estes, author of *Women Who Run with the Wolves*, says of the destruction that comes from not living from the authentic self:

> There is in its fiery and destructive centre a something that fuses fierceness to wisdom in the woman who has danced the cursed dance, who has lost herself and her creative life, ... and yet who has somehow held onto a word, a thought, an idea until she could escape her demon through a crack in time and live to tell about it.[1]

The loss of my creative self, and particularly, my writing self, was a blow too many. I wandered through the days almost without presence; waif-like, malnourished. Estes says of this lowest point of the low, that there is fecundity, hope: 'at bottom is the best soil to sow and grow something new'.[2]

In my previous existence, I had been connected to strings which restricted my movements; I was a marionette. Each time I fell down or was raised, I did so with those strings attached. I had never been free. Losing my creative self took me to the 'bottom', from where I could start anew. It was my opportunity to snap those strings.

Edith Eger says, 'the things that interrupt our lives, that stop us in our tracks, can also be catalysts for the emerging self, tools that show us a new way to be, that endow us with new vision.'[3]

Through the process of writing my way out of complete creative writing block and into a new writing practice, I found freedom. In choosing to write about domestic abuse, I uncovered truths, understandings, knowledge. The scales fell from my eyes. I was free of trying 'to be good while normalising the abnormal'.[4]

But this is not the end of the journey. Estes wisely states it is incorrect …

> to think that once we solve an issue it stays solved, that once we learn, we always remain conscious ever after … If we could realise that the work is to keep doing the work, we would be much more fierce and much more peaceful.[5]

Perhaps to 'keep doing the work' means maintaining vigilance in my words, expressions, gestures and behaviours so I no longer contribute to the problem, do not again become complicit. Sara Ahmed says, 'the hardest work can be recognising how one's own life is shaped by norms in ways that we did not realise, in ways that cannot simply be transcended.'[6]

On the journey of recovering my writing self, I gained clarity, understanding and recovery from the normalisation of domestic abuse. I now have voice. I now have wisdom.

THE WRITING PROJECT

Writing wisdom

Conclusion

Post-experiment writing

I commenced this research project in 2015. For years, I continued to be overwhelmed with court appearances that were emotionally, cognitively, and physically taxing, ongoing legal issues and, overriding these, fears for my personal safety. All while trying to maintain the pretence of normality when at work. All while playing the role I had been taught from birth: that I was fine, that everything was fine. Attempting to retrieve my lost personal writing practice was slow, arduous even, and initially, it appeared to offer little reward.

The writing experiments, with their guiding structure, were the key to my success. Supporting my approach to the experiments was an understanding of the nature of writing for the self. This meant that when I was ready, I was free to move away from reliance on the structure to more spontaneous writing.

It was in developing the supporting framework that I set myself up for success. Even so, I had to do the work, weather the disappointments, and pick myself up when I fell down. There were, too, great gaps created by a debilitating health condition. And yet, I persisted. What is there in life to demand our persistence and tenacity if not the goal of regaining our own sense of self? In the process, I rediscovered my voice, and gained agency. Through writing about domestic abuse, I learnt much about my individual experience, unearthing self-truths about my behaviours and beliefs, that, in the words of Clarissa Pinkola Estes, caused me to 'so drastically lose (my) way'.[1] Through writing, I could bring these into the light and name them. Later, in revisiting my writing, I was able to situate my personal experience within a broader social story.

If 'writing is a journey of self-discovery, one in which we construct through language a sense of self',[2] does losing the ability to express one's creative self through writing mean a loss of this sense of self? It did for me. My way to reconnect with my inner voice was through planned forays into the creative writing process. The supporting framework acknowledged who I was, how I saw the world and what I knew, so I could step with purpose into that creative writing process.

To embark on a journey is to take chances. I started this journey without a guide: no one had laid down a path for me to follow. It was, in many ways, a journey into the self. Recovering from loss, however, allows us to face life with new skills, to share our wisdom with others, to model success. I share the feeling of joy expressed by Virginia Woolf in her 1924 diary where she said, 'I can write and write and write now: the happiest feeling in the world'.[3]

I end this memoir with a piece written in the companionship of an online writing group. It received an honourable mention in *Kaleidoscope WoJo Reflections of Women's Journeys - What is your happy place contest*. I could write this story, and write many more for myself, because of this writing project.

CONCLUSION

My happy place (Friday, 20 November 2020)

I walk along the high street in Bulimba, that riverside gem of a leafy suburb so close to the ever-growing city of Brisbane, and yet, so removed. I am alone but not free of my troubles. To see me, you might be reminded of that character from Charlie Brown, the one that always had squiggly lines about him, indicating I think ... was it smell? For me, it is a pulsating cloud of detritus sitting always over my head. I imagine it looks like the obscured fight scene from an old-fashioned cartoon, where fists in motion can be seen protruding from a cloud of dust.

As I walk along, heavy under this cloud, I notice a bright patch of yellow to my right. My legs continue moving me forward, but my eyes are no longer fixed on the internal scene playing constantly in my mind.

I stop to look, I must, for I am drawn to the yellow on this grey day. There, on display in a window, is something bright.

I don't want to buy anything; I cannot bear the thought of having any more belongings. My future is uncertain. Any day, or so a Supreme Court judge has told me, he (the judge) can take away everything I own. Any day is a day that I and my rescue animals can made homeless.

I turn around, retrace my steps, and enter the store with intention. It is crowded with people, as is the way with second-hand bookstores on a rainy day.

I weave my way through and around the people, taking in the tall shelves packed with books. The shop is small and ill-shaped, bending around one edge of the building it is attached to. The aisles are narrow, the browsers reticent to make way.

Stand by, I cry out, if only in my mind, for I am on a mission. I will not be deterred.

Persistence moves me on. In the far window, I locate the source of the brightness that attracted me. It is a children's book: *The Singing Hat*.[4] I reach out to touch the bright yellow cover, and now I notice the bird. The bird in the nest on the head of the man on the cover of the book.

I sit in the window and gently turn the pages, lost to all around me. Forgotten also is the heavy cloud that hangs above me. I am engaging in reading for pleasure, ludic reading, 'the experience of being lost in a book, in absorption or entrancement'.[5] To be released, for just a few moments, from the burdens that never leave me, is to be blessed with a moment of grace. I buy the book, and tenderly hold it against my heart as I return to my car.

That evening, before my nightly battle with the demons that invade my sleep, I open the book and read. I hear the bird in the nest on the head of the man. I hear her tweet:

Tweet, tweet, twitter, twit

I admire the man and his conviction to do no harm, when it would be so easy to relinquish all responsibility.

I ponder his query to a former friend, 'But what would you do?'

This is serious stuff, really, what would I do?

I empathise with what it means to lose people we think are friends because we find ourselves in circumstances not of our own making.

I worry about the bird, its vulnerability, its fragility, its trust in the man with the nest on his head.

CONCLUSION

While I read, my concerns, my worries, my feelings, are for the characters in a book with a yellow cover, and for those moments, my concerns, my worries, are not for myself.

For weeks I read this book every night before I wearily give in to the demons that await me in my sleep. These few minutes' reading are a gift, a moment away from the journey that I am on, that I can't get off, that I must see through to the end because there is no optional exit.

In psychology, this type of escapism might be classified as an 'avoidant strategy', a way of not dealing with one's problems. I see that pure enjoyment of reading and becoming lost in a children's book as an act of kindness to myself, a brief moment of respite from unremitting pressure. It became my happy place, that book, *The Singing Hat*. The one about the man with a bird in a nest on his head. It now stands on display in my own bookcase, a constant reminder of the bright sparks and glimpses of light that are there, even in the darkest of places.

THE WRITING PROJECT

Writing whenever, wherever, I need

Notes

INTRODUCTION

1. United Nations, *What is Domestic Abuse?* 2020. www.un.org/en/coronavirus/what-is-domestic-abuse
2. Y. Khan, 'Domestic violence or domestic abuse? Why terminology matters', *Women's Agenda*, 2019. https://womensagenda.com.au/uncategorised/
3. *Personal Safety 2016*, Australian Bureau of Statistics, 2017. www.Abs.Gov.Au/ausstats/abs@.Nsf/mf/4906.0
4. *Family, Domestic and Sexual Violence in Australia: Continuing the National Story*, Australian Institute of Health and Welfare, 2019. doi: 25816/5ebcc837fa7ea

CHAPTER 1

1. S. Poff, *Regimentation: A Predictor of Writer's Block and Writing Apprehension* (Doctoral thesis), University of Southern California, 2004.
2. R. Boice, 'Writing blocks and tacit knowledge', *The Journal of Higher Education*, 64 no. 1, 1993.
3. Da Capo Press, 2012.

NOTES

4 Page 61, above.
5 As above.
6 R. Freeman & K. Le Rossignon, 'Writer-as-narrator: Engaging the debate around the (un)reliable narrator in memoir and the personal essay', *TEXT* 19 no. 1, 2015. www.textjournal.com.au/april15/freeman_lerossignol.htm
7 I included more recent statistics when editing this chapter in 2022. I believe that current information is more informative to both the reader and the discussion.
8 Australian Institute of Health and Welfare, *Family, Domestic and Sexual Violence in Australia, 2018.* www.aihw.gov.au/reports/family-domestic-and-sexual-violence/family-domestic-sexual-violence-australia-2019/contents/summary
9 Australian Institute of Health and Welfare, *Examination of Hospital Stays due to Family and Domestic Violence 2010-11 to 2018-9.* www.aihw.gov.au/reports/family-domestic-and-sexual-violence/examination-of-hospital-stays-due-to-family-and-do/summary
10 Australian Institute of Criminology, *International Violence Against Women Survey (Australian Component), December 2002 - June 2003.* https://apo.org.au/node/4140
11 As above.
12 L. Fahey, *Three Days in A Refuge*, ABC News. www.abc.net.au/news/2015-07-08/three-days-in-domestic-violence-refuge/6503954?nw=0
13 As above.
14 Women's Information and Referral Exchange Inc, 2015. www.wire.org.au/stalking/

NOTES

CHAPTER 1 REFLECTIONS

1. I wrote this piece in response to reading the following: *What is Trauma Bonding?* Parents Against Child Exploitation, 2022. https://paceuk.info/child-sexual-exploitation/what-is-trauma-bonding/
2. N. LePera, *How to do the Work: Recognise your Patterns, Heal from your Past, and Create your Self*, Orion Spring, 2021.

CHAPTER 2

1. S. Trenoweth, *Fury: Women Write about Sex, Power and Violence*, Hardie Books, 2015.
2. Page 229. Entry for 28 May, 1929 in *The Diary of Virginia Woolf, Volume III: 1925–1930*, Hogarth Press, 1980.
3. N. Wolff, *A Woman's Place*. www.feministezine.com/feminist/postfeminism/A-Womans-Place.html

CHAPTER 2 REFLECTIONS

1. Page 965. M. Emirbayer & A. Mische, 'What is agency?' *The American Journal of Sociology* 103 no. 4, 1998.
2. My own piece, written and added in 2020, inspired by reading B. Minchinton & S. Hayes, 'Brothels and sex workers: Variety, complexity and change in nineteenth-century Little Lon, Melbourne', *Australian Historical Studies* 51 no. 2, 2020.
3. L.M. Ahearn, 'Language and agency, *Annual Review of Anthropology* 30 no. 1, 2001.
4. A 'witness' described my scream for my life as a 'squeak', adding, she thought I was squeaking because I'd seen a mouse. I've noted, when watching news reports of violent attacks on women in their homes, that neighbours describe their screams as 'squeals', likening them to children's play.

NOTES

5 A. Cabraaal, *When I Write, I Write for Myself*. https://researchwhisperer.org/2020/04/14/when-i-write-i-write-for-myself/
6 Extract from the field notes I wrote in conjunction with the writing experiments.
7 Page 33. C. Vaughan, et al., 'Promoting community-led responses to violence against immigrant and refugee women in metropolitan and regional Australia', *The ASPIRE Project: State of Knowledge Paper*, Paper 7, Australia's National Research Organisation for Women's Safety, 2015. https://d2rn9gno7zhxqg.cloudfront.net/wp-content/uploads/2019/02/19024843/12_1.2-Landscapes-ASPIRE-web.pdf

CHAPTER 3

1 L. Carroll, first published in 1865.
2 D. Halverson, *Writing Young Adult Fiction for Dummies*, Wiley Publishing, 2011.
3 Puffin, 1992.

CHAPTER 3 REFLECTIONS

1 There is much published on this topic. For example, see A.E. Street, et al., 'Impact of childhood traumatic events, trauma-related guilt, and avoidant coping strategies on PTSD symptoms in female survivors of domestic violence', *Journal of Traumatic Stress* 18 no. 3, 2005.
2 E.D. Krause, et al., 'Avoidant coping and PTSD symptoms related to domestic violence exposure: A longitudinal study', *Journal of Traumatic Stress* 21 no. 1, 2008.

NOTES

CHAPTER 4

1. 1867.
2. Page 69. D. Hanauer, 'Multicultural moments in poetry: The importance of the unique', *The Canadian Modern Language Review* 60 no. 1, 2003.
3. Picador, 2000.
4. S. Davidow & P. Williams, Palgrave, 2016.
5. Picador, 1999.
6. Page 101, above.
7. The French man I was married to suffered from delusions of superiority. According to him, Australians are peasants.

CHAPTER 4 REFLECTIONS

1. Pages 2-3. *Embodied Inquiry: Writing, Living and Being through the Body*, Brill/Sense, 2016.

CHAPTER 5

1. *Little Black Book of Stories*, Vintage, 2004.
2. I returned to Byatt and Carter's stories once I had completed writing my fairy tale. I then rewrote the discussion, which now more adequately reflects the notions I could not explain clearly in the earlier stages of scripting this chapter.
3. *The Bloody Chamber and Other Stories*, Penguin, 1993.
4. Page 73. B.J. Zimmerman & R. Risemberg, 'Becoming a self-regulated writer: A social cognitive perspective', *Contemporary Educational Psychology* 22 no.1, 1997.
5. V. Nelson, *Writer's Block and How to Use it*, Writer's Digest Books, 1985.

NOTES

CHAPTER 5 REFLECTIONS

1. Page 237. C.P. Estes, *Women Who Run with the Wolves: Contacting the Power of the Wild Woman*, Rider, 1992.
2. Page 14. Penguin, 1992.
3. Page 244. Estes, as above.

CHAPTER 6

1. S.W. Porges, 'The polyvagal perspective', *Biological Psychology* 74 no.2, 2007.
2. As above.
3. S. Joseph, *What Doesn't Kill Us: The New Psychology of Posttraumatic Growth*, Piatkus, 2011.
4. S.W. Porges, 'The vagal paradox: A polyvagal solution', *Comprehensive Psychoneuroendocrinology* 16, 2023.
5. P.A. Williams, 'Autobiographical research in a post-traumatic body: A retrospective risk analysis. *TEXT* 21 Special 42, 2017. doi.org/10.52086/001c.25897
6. Page 5, as above.
7. Penguin, 2015.
8. A. Konig, *Disclosure and Health: Enhancing the Benefits of Trauma Writing through Response Training* (Doctoral Thesis), Virginia Commonwealth University, 2011.
9. M. Giles, 'Writing trauma', *Overland* 12, 2016. https://overland.org.au/2016/12/writing-trauma/
10. J. Littrell, 'Expression of emotion: When it causes trauma and when it helps', *Journal of Evidence-Based Social Work* 6 no. 3, 2009. 'Reappraisal' here means assisting the victim to change her thoughts and responses to the trauma.
11. W. Ings, 'Narcissus and the muse: Supervisory implications of autobiographical, practice-led PhD design theses', *Qualitative Research* 14 no.6, 2014.

12 As above.
13 Giles, as above.
14 Page 1319. R. Rosenblum, 'Postponing trauma: The dangers of telling', *The International Journal of Psychoanalysis* 90, 2009. I note that this researcher interviews and discusses survivors of the most brutal, human-instigated abuses.

CHAPTER 6 REFLECTIONS

1 B. van der Kolk, *The Body Keeps the Score: Mind, Brain and Body in the Transformation of Trauma*, Penguin, 2014.

CHAPTER 7

1 S. Tamas, 'Writing and righting trauma: Troubling the autoethnographic voice', *Forum Qualitative Sozialforschung / Forum: Qualitative Social Research* 10 no. 1, 2009. doi.org/10.17169/fqs-10.1.1211.

CHAPTER 7 REFLECTIONS

1 Page 7. C. Snowber, *Embodied Inquiry: Writing, Living and Being through the Body*, Brill / Sense, 2016.
2 Page 245. C.P. Estes, *Women Who Run with the Wolves: Contacting the Power of the Wild Woman*, Rider, 1992.
3 Page 132. 'Imagine how many people you can help with your testimony', T. Navarro, *Kintsugi: Embrace Your Imperfections and Find Happiness – The Japanese Way*, Yellow Kite, 2018.

NOTES

CHAPTER 8

1   1697.
2   V. Nelson, *Writer's Block and How to Use It*, Writer's Digest Books, 1985; D. Murray, 'The essential delay: When writers block isn't', in *When a Writer Can't Write: Studies in Writer's Block and Other Composing Problems*, Guilford Press, 1985.
3   'On Flow', in S. Perry, *Ursula K. Le Guin's Strong Opinions about Writing in Flow: Understanding Flow May Be More Complex Than You Think*, 2018. www.psychologytoday.com/au/blog/creating-in-flow/201803/ursula-k-le-guins-strong-opinions-about-writing-in-flow
4   This idea is expanded on by M. Warner, *From Beast to Blonde: On Fairy Tales and Their Tellers*, Farrar, Straus & Giroux, 1994. See Chapter 15.
5   Page 244, as above.
6   See the UNICEF report, *Behind Closed Doors: The Impact of Domestic Violence on Children*, 2006 for details. www.medbox.org/document/behind-closed-doors-the-impact-of-domestic-violence-on-children#GO

CHAPTER 8 REFLECTIONS

1   Page 219. C.P. Estes, *Women Who Run with the Wolves: Contacting the Power of the Wild Woman*, Rider, 1992.
2   J. Herman, *Trauma and Recovery: The Aftermath of Violence – From Domestic Abuse to Political Terror*, Basic Books, 2015.

NOTES

CHAPTER 9 REFLECTIONS

1. She says on page 7, 'I need to make my voice match my words'. 'Writing and righting trauma: Troubling the autoethnographic voice: Forum', *Qualitative Social Research* 10 no. 1, 2009. doi.org/10.17169/fqs-10.1.1211
2. As above.

CHAPTER 10

1. Picador, Pan McMillian, 2001.
2. This is not the case throughout the book. She does say, 'I hate writing' and calls it a sickness on page 37.
3. Page 181. J. Owen, et al., 'Truth troubles', *Qualitative Inquiry* 15 no. 1, 2009.

CHAPTER 10 REFLECTIONS

1. Page 159. Penguin, 1992.
2. ABC News, Fri 24 Sep 2021. www.abc.net.au/news/2021-09-24/qld-murder-becomes-manslaughter-in-retrial-peniamina/100489066
3. I use these seemingly extreme examples because I have lived in a country where these actions, occurring on a daily basis, were simply ignored by passers-by.

NOTES

CHAPTER 11

1. Page 10. E. Bailey, *The Sound of a Wild Snail Eating*, Algonquin Books, 2010.
2. As above.
3. As above.
4. University of Chicago Press, 1946.
5. R. Mahoney, Black Bay Books, 2007.
6. A. Piper, Melbourne University Press, 2012.
7. S. Henshaw, Constable & Robinson, 2014.
8. I am also engaging in other forms of creative expression that I could not for that decade: ad lib cooking, daydreaming, gardening, decorating.
9. Page 23. *Living a Feminist Life*, Duke University Press, 2017.
10. Page 81. F. Vera-Gray, *The Right Amount of Panic: How Women Trade Freedom for Safety*, Policy Press, 2018.
11. Penguin, 2014.
12. Page 324. K. Eason & N. Hodges, 'Reading contemporary female body modification as a site of Cixous' l'écriture féminine', *Fashion Theory* 15 no. 3, 2011.

CHAPTER 11 REFLECTIONS

1. Page 23. S. Ahmed, *Living a Feminist Life*, Duke University Press, 2017.
2. *The Empathy Exams: Essays*, Graywolf, 2014.
3. Conclusion. S. Ahmed, as above.
4. Page 45. b. hooks, *Remembered Rapture: The Writer at Work*, Holt, 1999.

NOTES

CHAPTER 12

1. E.B. White, Puffin Books, 1952/2003.
2. Penguin Random House, 2017.
3. Simon & Schuster, 2018.

CHAPTER 12 REFLECTIONS

1. Page 220. C.P. Estes, *Women Who Run with the Wolves: Contacting the Power of the Wild Woman*, Rider, 1992.
2. As above.
3. Page 26. *The Gift: 12 Lessons to Save Your Life*, Rider, 2020.
4. Page 245. Estes, as above.
5. As above.
6. Page 43. *Living a Feminist Life*, Duke University Press, 2017

CONCLUSION

1. Page 220. *Women Who Run with the Wolves: Contacting the Power of the Wild Woman*, Rider, 1992.
2. Page 229. J. Armstrong, 'Writing as self-invention', in *The Road to Somewhere: A Creative Writing Companion*, 2nd edition, Palgrave MacMillian, 2013.
3. *A Room of One's Own*, Wiley Blackwell, 2015/1929.
4. T. Riddle, Viking, 2000.
5. V. Nell, 'The psychology of reading for pleasure: Needs and gratifications', *Reading Research Quarterly* 23 no. 1, 1988.

NOTES

Create for yourself and your self